EARLY PRAISE
SPIRITUAL GR

"This book is a magnificent exhale for the soul. Many sincere seekers become bamboozled by spiritual teachers who suggest that we ignore our feelings, numb our bodies, and violate our intuition in the name of enlightenment. But Jeff Brown humbly offers an alternative, even rebellious, viewpoint. With exquisite sensitivity and compassion, he acknowledges that we can't wake up without grounding our self-realization into our feeling, sensing human bodies. I am a voracious student of spiritual teaching, but Jeff Brown is a spiritual teacher I truly trust, marrying incisive, almost surgical truth with supreme kindness in a way that enlivens your spirit and makes you feel your heart. He is like a scalpel with a spoonful of sugar."

—LISSA RANKIN, NY Times bestselling author of
Mind Over Medicine

"Unabashedly written from his heart and guts, Jeff Brown's *Spiritual Graffiti* is a brave, bold, and very real offering of what it means to be human. Filled with raw truth, inspiration and plenty of insights into the path of awakening, this book is sure to serve those well who read it."

ualist
Mind

"Jeff Brown's words are the much needed love-splattered slap to our wearied New Age-filled heads. In *Spiritual Graffiti* we get a glimpse into the way that light and positivity alone will never reveal to us the mystery of both our humanity and our Godhood. Through his decades of deep personal inquiry, Jeff reveals his painful and potent intimacy with his own darkness as a pathway to revelation. *Spiritual Graffiti* is a deep-dive into the soul of one man, and yet a mirror for all who find themselves on the journey towards 'enREALment.' I'm a forever fan."

—KATIE SILCOX, spiritual teacher and NY Times bestselling author of *Healthy Happy Sexy: Ayurveda Wisdom for Modern Women*

"*Spiritual Graffiti* sprays us with a rebel call to deeper love. Jeff Brown's words masterfully woke me up, pissed me off, and then openly seduced me back into my own heart. He invites us to drop the pretense, befriend our shadow and find God-Goddess in the very earth under our fingernails. This little book offers a banquet of soul nourishment and tangible guidance on how to be more alive in walking our own truth. The messiness of life and love makes a little more sense looking through this sacred lens. Bravo.

—LISA SCHRADER, Author, Coach and Founder of AwakeningShakti.com

"*Spiritual Graffiti* sizzles with courage. With a fearless pen, Jeff Brown inscribes his unique wisdom in practical, succinct, and heart-centered language that sagaciously calls out the negligence of today's New Age movement and walks us boldly to our highest callings."

—SUSAN FRYBORT, author of *Hope is a Traveler*

"Jeff Brown's words touch a place deep in my heart. They remind my heart of many things she knows but often resists---that none of us are flawed or broken, we are beautifully Whole just as we are, and within each of us is the stunning courage to live a radically authentic, awake, and open-hearted life. Each and every page of *Spiritual Graffiti* is a nourishing treasure for the soul. I highly recommend this powerful book."

—JUNA MUSTAD MILANO, co-founder of
DailyRelationship.com

"Jeff Brown's latest work is a testimonial to the soul. His writing is at the edge, breaking through the cosmic and cultural barriers to reveal things in an entirely new way. He understands the vital importance to converse about the soul in every aspect of life. This makes him a modern day Troubadour. A must read for Divine Lovers everywhere!"

—ANAIYA SOPHIA, author of *Sacred Sexual Union*
and co-author of *Womb Wisdom*

"*Spiritual Graffiti* allows readers the experience of truly feeling heard and seen for their difficult experiences. Jeff is a master of sharing real and raw truths that most are often too scared to share. In doing so, he gives readers the feeling that they are not alone, and gives readers the motivation to rise from the ashes and soar. It is inspiring, soulful, and a must read for anyone on a path to true soul growth."

—CHRISTINE GUTIERREZ, Psychotherapist
(www.christineg.tv)

SPIRITUAL GRAFFITI

Jeff Brown

ENREALMENT PRESS
TORONTO, CANADA

Published by Enrealment Press
PO Box 64
Acton, Ontario
Canada L7J 2M2

Cover photo by Nerijus Juras/Shutterstock
Author photos by Paul Hemrend and Tarini Bresgi
Cover and book design by Allyson Woodrooffe (go-word.com)
Printed in the USA

Library and Archives Canada Cataloguing in Publication
Brown, Jeff, 1962-, author
Spiritual graffiti /Jeff Brown.

Poems.
ISBN 978-0-9808859-9-6 (paperback)
ISBN 978-0-9947843-0-8 (pdf)

I. Title.
PS8603.R68394S65 2015   C811'.6   C2015-905803-1

I dedicate this book to my mother, Barbara Marcia Brown, who transitioned this summer. My greatest teacher, my deepest challenge, the fire of overcoming in my belly. We were a perfect match, dear one. I shall meet you there, and we shall revel in our accomplishment.

Ma. Nothing to hide, now. Nothing to be angry about, now. Nothing to deny, now. I can finally feel all of your love. All of it. Vast as an ocean, tender as a reed. You just couldn't show it in your bodysuit, but it was always there, longing to be revealed. It's okay if it took death to reveal it, it wanted to be seen. It wanted to be shared. It's a pleasure to finally meet you. Ma.

Note to the Reader

Note on the word "God": When used in this book, the word "God" is not a linear, limited or limiting definition. It is not guilt or shame associated, not religiously affiliated, not affixed to any particular doctrine.

It is an open-ended term that can be interpreted and applied in whatever way you personally relate to and identify with it: Divinity, Higher Power, Goddess, Nature, Unity Consciousness, Source, Truth, Infinity, Wholeness, to name only a few. Whatever feels true for you. The author is himself an avid explorer of the God concept, and his perspective changes as his experiences inform and expand his consciousness. What he identified as God through a more individualized lens, is entirely different from how he came to understand God through the eyes of love. Perhaps God morphs as we morph, or, perhaps we are seeking an understanding far beyond our comprehension.

A Call to Authenticity

Dear Reader: Although I use the word 'spiritual' in the title, make no mistake as to my meaning. By spiritual, I do not mean anything that is exclusively transcendent, etheric, or blissful. I don't mean anything steeped in artificial forgiveness, wishful thinking, radical detachment, ego-bashing. By spiritual, I am not referencing a consciousness that disparages our personal stories and 'pain-bodies', as though our painful stories are distinct from who we really are. And I don't mean meditation as the primary path to the 'Kingdom' of God. No, not at all.

I have been around the 'spiritual' community for many years. Where at first, I loved the seeming gentleness, the unboundaried openness, the reality re-frames, the earnest quest for an enlightened state, I have now come to believe that much of what passes for 'spiritual' is not spiritual at all. It is actually an attempt to bypass deeper truths and issues, and to defend against the difficult elements of the human experience. It is a half-baked reality, eliminating many of the nuances, facets and dimensions of this wondrous human existence.

When I look around the present-day spiritual arena, I see many lies and evasions: gurus with compromised integrity; emotionally flat-lined spiritual teachers who have merely fled their unresolved issues; and seekers who have chosen——sometimes quite consciously—to adhere to simplistic frameworks and techniques in an effort to sidestep their challenges, concerns and the healthy friction intrinsic to life.

It is true that life can be tremendously difficult, but in our quest to rise above the human fray, we have actually taken ourselves further away from the place of resolution: our down-to-earth, real-time, embodied experience. When we bypass our unresolved emotions, when we deny our uncomfortable truths, we actually delay our own evolution. Because at their heart, repressed emotions are unactualized spiritual lessons. And our truth-aches are a beacon of divine possibility, illuminating the next steps on our journey towards wholeness. The opportunity for transformation is right here, in the heart of the everything.

What I once respectfully honored as a new age for humanity, I now refer to as the 'New Cage Movement', as I witness seekers fleeing their humanness—and opportunities for deeper transformation—in droves. I use this term to describe the ungrounded, dangerous and simplistic elements of the New Age movement, including but not limited to: wishful thinking mantras, spiritual bypass and premature forgiveness practices, superficial healing techniques, the perpetual denial of common sense realities, and the insistence on inflated, fantastical perspectives—'Everything is an illusion,' 'It's all perfect,' 'There are no victims,' 'Anger is a sub-standard emotion,' 'All judgments are bad,' 'You chose your every experience and circumstance,' 'Everything that happens is meant-to-be,' 'Your personal identifi-cations are inherently false,' 'Just ask the universe for what you want...,' 'Everything you see and feel is a re-flection of you,' 'There is no one to blame,' 'The ego is the enemy,' etc. These perspectives have their place in certain circumstances, but taken too far—as they often are—become a prison of their own making, locking hu-manity in with its unresolved pain.

The real dawning of a new age for humanity re-quires that we let go of the ungrounded notion that real spirituality exists independent of our human experience. This is the big lie, perpetuated by masters of self-avoid-ance masquerading as enlightened masters. Yes, we are spiritual beings having a human experience. But we are also human beings having a spiritual experience. They are one and the same. All too often what is presented as non-duality/'unity consciousness' is something that has removed everything uncomfortable from the uni-fied field. You can't have All-Oneness if you discard the ego, the emotions, the stories, the identity, the body, the psyche and the self. That may be unity for a robot, but not for a human being. Presence is a whole being experience. And detachment is a tool—it's not a life.

The irony is that what motivates the quest for pseudo non-duality is often the unresolved elements themselves. The denial of the ego is motivated by the unhealthy aspects of ego. The diminishment of the emotional body is motivated by the unhealed emotional body. The suggestion that everything is an illusion is motivated by a fear of reality. And the belief that witnessing the pain-body evaporates it is motivated by the pain-body run amok. Witnessing our pain doesn't dissipate it. It strengthens it. If you want to dissipate it, get inside it and work it through, until it is thoroughly mended. And when it is truly healed, it will both create a richer, fuller life and reveal its essential nature—grist for the soul mill itself. The granules of glory that grew us closer to the Godself. How can we grow without this fodder for our expansion; the soil of our lived-in experience?

It is my view that what we have come to call 'spiritual' is actually little more than a single-threaded consciousness. Individuals become effective at one state or practice—skilled witnessers, expert meditators, head-tripping conceptualists, Olympic champions of story re-frame and premature forgiveness—and they make the mistake of calling that limited state spiritual. In fact, spirituality IS reality. The most spiritual experience is the one that encompasses multiple realms in any given moment. Sitting on a meditation cushion witnessing emotions float past is not inherently more spiritual than sitting at a donut shop eating a double chocolate, while watching the world go by. The deeper question is where our attention is and how fully we are embracing all elements of the moment. If we expand our definition of spirituality to include an integration of all aspects of reality—including the processing of emotional debris and psychological issues, practical challenges, money management, familial/ancestral imprinting, dealing with the world—then those who have perfected Eastern and meditative threads of practice are not nearly as spiritual as day to day people who have learned how to live in the world in a heartfelt, balanced and grounded way. The real master, if mastery is even possible, is a Master of Enrealment, one who is inclusively connected to all that is human—joy and sorrow, shopping list and unity consciousness, fresh mangoes and stale bread—in any given moment. We are not just the light, or the mind, or the emptiness, or perpetual positivity. We are the everything. It's ALL God, even the dust that falls off our awakening hearts.

This is not simply a conceptual issue. It is far more

significant than that. These narrow definitions of spirituality actually have hard-core, real-life consequences. For example, I spent considerable time around a group of self-proclaimed teachers who understood spirituality in exclusively vertical terms. Their idea of unity consciousness did not include anything horizontal or heartfelt, such as human relationships, healthy sexuality and intimacy, their connection to the world around them. It was, instead, entirely a function of their connection to something above them: a heavenly God, the Big Daddy Creator in the sky who they accessed alone on a meditative head-trip into the eternal emptiness. Meanwhile, they were busy using and abusing various women. When I asked them how they could claim to be enlightened while behaving without integrity in their personal lives, their response was always along the same lines: "Morality and Enlightenment exist independent of each other." And there it was—you can be enlightened while doing damage to others. You can be enlightened while doing damage to the planet. You can be enlightened when you are bypassing your childhood wounds. You can be enlightened while being a sociopath. So much for the heart as a pathway to realization. Over time, I came to understand that these grifters in guru garb were not actually seeking an enlightened consciousness. They were seeking a way to bypass their earthly issues, while stoking the unhealthy ego. They were seeking a new and improved identity as a spiritual 'somebody.' EnBullshitment, at its truest.

Let's take it one step further and consider the possibility that the way we define spirituality is actually a life and death matter. Because it is. I have known a few individuals in my immediate circle who turned to various New Cage and detachment-driven philosophies to find relief from the emotional pain they carried. These approaches served them for a time, but invariably they came crashing back to earth, leaving them even less prepared to deal with reality than before. All those years spent staring at the pain-body across the room while their shadow grew larger, congealing into weapons that eventually turned inward against the self. I personally knew one trauma-survivor who was so seduced by the mantras of the ungrounded spirituality movement ('story is illusion', 'suffering is illusion', 'trauma is part of the cosmic plan.') that he angrily turned against the psychotherapist that had kept him afloat for many years. Unfortunately, his depression came back with a fierceness, demanding attention, and he no longer had the tools or support structures to manage it. Shortly thereafter, he hung himself. He simply couldn't deal with 'the now' because he was still crippled by 'the then.' What he needed was more healing, not more self-avoidance techniques. Prayers for those who have been led astray.

Let there be no doubt that models that lead people away from the healing of the heart do not serve humanity. Unfortunately, the New Cage and spiritual bypass movements prey on trauma survivors in an effort to sell product and build their followings. And the irony is everywhere. In their insistence on non-judgment, they judge. In their emphasis on pain as an illusion, they create more pain. In their emphasis on premature forgiveness, they delay authentic forgiveness. In their insistence on non-victimhood where someone has clearly been abused, they victimize. In their desire to bypass reality, they make reality a more difficult place to manage. And on it goes... The oppressive nature of ungrounded spiritualities, where dissociation masquerades as bliss and everyone comes crashing back to earth with a hard and heavy thud.

After the pseudo-positivity falls away, after our 'illusory' story reminds us that it is deeply real, after the neglected shadow returns with a vengeance, we need to get support. Not from television soulebrities selling enlightenment by the bushel, but from grounded healers and therapists who understand the nature of sustainable transformation. When the truth hits the fan, we don't need mantras of self-avoidance. We don't need dissociation techniques. We don't need exorbitantly priced quick-fix workshops. We don't need Eastern wisdoms that negate the psyche. We don't need 'enlightenment' without affect. We need to be seen and supported. We need to be held in the heart of compassion. We need to heal. Better we remain down on earth and do the real work to transform our challenges into the gold at their heart. Healing and healthy boundaries before Oneness. Truth is the gateway to the moment.

I mean, really. If we are going to claim to be in a unified field, at the very least, the emotional body should be included in the equation. If we are expanding in our consciousness, every element of the human experience comes along for the ride, and that includes the personality portal. Head-tripping and perpetual witnessing are not the furthest reaches of human expansion. That is a patriarchal version of spirituality that is not serving this planet. Non-duality that bypasses the pain-body, the unresolveds, the ego, the body and the identity is not unity. It's just a drug trip. And there's nothing more dual than that.

The problem does not lie in the dualities themselves—for we are surely in them for a reason—but in our inability to learn the lessons at their heart. Pretending we are not fragmented does not make us whole. It is only through a growing interface with our real-life experiences and challenges—the School of Heart

Knocks—that we can evolve towards a deeper spiritual life. After all, spirituality is not all fairies and unicorns. It is reality, in all its nuanced complexity and intricacy. It's time for a version of non-duality that is relational, emotionally vital and pulsing with energy. Let's show up for all of it, and call THAT spirituality.

At its heart, this book is a call to action. A call to inclusivity. A call to embodiment, enheartenment, enrealment. A call to authenticity. A call to healing the broken heart of humanity. A call to a spirituality that is rooted, vital and relational. A call to common sense.

This book is also a call to spiritual activism. We have become conditioned to believe that spirituality is only a gentle way, not one that includes confrontation, even confrontation of a benevolent form: the way of the spiritual warrior. It's time to let that nonsense go and embrace the reality that not all positive change will happen gently. Not a chance—not yet. The darkness will not give way that easily. And I am not simply talking about activism with respect to the issues of the day. I am also talking about activism with respect to the so-called spiritual community itself. If you look closely, even the spiritual scene has become highly politicized. I had always imagined spirituality as a quest for truth. Not everyone agrees. There is a lot invested in the spiritual community in having particular opinions protected, not unlike many controlling political and financial systems. A form of spiritual fascism develops, one that benefits only a small few. If you call out the lying guru, you are met with the 'no gossip' mantra. If you shake your fist in rage, you are reminded that spirituality does not include anger. If you call out the detachment addicts, they detach from your connection. If you call out the New Cagers, you are shamed and isolated. Repression is an industry and the ungrounded spiritual community is one of its primary merchants. Let's spend our hard-earned karma elsewhere.

At the end of the day, when all the other debates have been resolved, we will be left with one: Human Consciousness. That is, what is an inclusive consciousness? What does it mean to be truly here? What does it mean to be wholly human? What ways of being reflect and honor our divine nature? If we don't embrace that inquiry, if we shun it in the name of soft touch spirituality, we will obstruct and distort our collective expansion. We will imprison ourselves in our own separateness. And many will be led astray, walking a path that is not truly their own. To avoid that, we must invite a conscious scrutinization now. We must challenge consciousness models. We must call out the lie wherever we see it. And we must let go of the idea that there is someone out there who has it all figured out. If they tell you that they have, walk the other way. They may have a worthwhile offering, but they are not enlightened masters. They are not realized beings, no matter what stories you are told of their great spiritual abilities. Awakening is a relative experience, one opening after another, from sole to soul... Let the debates begin. Better we bravely and boldly speak our truths and let the karmic chips fall where they may.

And let's not forget to shine the light of truth in our own direction. Spiritual activism begins at home: Where are we being dishonest? Where are we misleading ourselves and others? Where are we bypassing our shadow? Where is there incongruence between our inner lives and our outer manifestation? Where are we not moving from sacred purpose? Where are we not true to path?

I have tremendous faith in humanity. I see a world of profound, bountiful possibility. But that faith is not blind. It's not going to be easy to meet ourselves where we truly live. But we can, and we will, once we decide that we are willing to do the real work to get here. Not the distracted here, not the story-bashing here, not the superior floating-above here, not the pain-body avoidant here, but the inclusive here. To get here, we have to come back into our bodies and heal the individual and collective heart. With our hearts closed and broken, we cannot be present. We cannot be spiritual. We cannot grow forward. To enhearten this mad world, we must prioritize emotional healing and transformation. It all begins and ends with the heart. We must encourage engaging in the therapeutic work that clears the debris that obstructs us. We must recognize that our emotional and spiritual lives are indistinguishable from each other. And we must stop hiding our love for each other, for ourselves, and for this remarkable planet, under a bushel of shame. There is nothing to hide, here. It's all God—every tear, every meal, every mantra, every breath—and it is love that reveals Her.

– Jeff Brown
Montréal, Canada
September 27, 2015

SPIRITUAL GRAFFITI

It's not about someone stealing our heart. It's about restoring its aliveness. It's about softening its armor. It's about filling it up with light. When real love enters, it doesn't take anything from us. It gifts us with the everything.

I am so tired of how hard we are on ourselves. Not attractive enough, not smart enough, not cool enough, not purpose-full enough, not spiritual enough, not flexible enough, not creative enough, not rich enough, not happy enough, not healthy enough, not sexy enough, not wise enough. It's like a collective shame-fest that begins when we are born and continues until we die. So much magnificent life is lost when it is swept under a mountain of shame. Billions of us walking around convinced we are not 'something enough.' We are missing the point. Just staying alive on this planet is a great achievement, demanding that we sift through all of the 'not-enough' inner chatter to find reason to go on. How about if we begin every day with an 'I am enough' meditation? Let's begin right now: I am enough! I am enough. I AM ENOUGH.

Being a sensitive person can be a confusing, complicated thing in this still harsh world. It feels intuitively right to open, to feel, to enhearten our daily life, but the world is still vibrating at a more armored and edgy place. It is not yet attuned to the ways of the open heart. So what to do? We don't want to deaden our capacity to feel, but if we feel too much, we get run over by an often heartless world. I have found my best answer in three places... Selective Attachment: carefully discerning between positive and negative individuals and environments, and only attaching to those people and places that can hold our tender heart safe; Strong Energetic Boundaries: being physically and emotionally charged, so that we can more effectively repel unwelcome energies; Conscious Armoring: learning how to put on armor when necessary to manage the world and difficult situations, and, consciously removing it when it is no longer needed. If we cultivate these practices, we stand a much better chance of preserving our sensitivity. Once we lose it, we lose our connection to the moment altogether. Here's to a sensitive way of being! What a courageous path.

Some people feel that they're being good friends, or good partners, when they give without ever asking for help. The ones who identify themselves as 'selfless givers.' But what they don't realize is that they are actually limiting the depths of the connection by keeping it a one-way street. They are stealing opportunities to get closer, to deepen in intimacy. Because when we deny the other person the chance to help us, we never taste the vulnerability of receiving. And they are prevented from experiencing the delights of being there for someone they love. Giving *and* receiving tightens bonds.

Compassion. It's not just a word. It's a way of being. It's not just a concept. It's love in action. It's not just something we conveniently practice. It's something we consistently embody. Compassion for those who are struggling. Compassion for our shared humanness. Compassion for the courage it takes to make it through. Unity begins and ends with compassion. I see me in you, I see you in me, and I want us to live from love together.

Some people need to create a nightmare far worse than the one they came from before they will go back and heal their early wounds. We see this in trauma survivors all the time. They pile hell upon hell, until they have only two choices—die, or heal the wounds they are fleeing. I used to find this confusing, but I no longer do. Sometimes the first hell was so bloody bad that it takes a far worse hell to uncover it. Bows to those who choose to heal their hells, after so many years on the run. Bows to those courageous beings who give reality a try before they have any evidence that it will serve them. If this isn't courage, I don't know what is.

A true master follows her own footprints, encoded within before arriving in this incarnation. Someone else may remind him, someone else may empower him, but no one else can possibly know the unique contours of his own true-path. Since you are the only one living in your temple, only you can know its scriptures and interpretive structure. The next step is right there inside you, divinely imprinted on the souls of your feet.

Those who condemn another's sexual orientation merely reveal the absence of depth in their own sexual lives. Because when you have had the highest form of sexual experience—one that is soul-sourced and soul-driven—you immediately recognize that gender is entirely irrelevant. The soul doesn't care about body parts. It simply loves what it loves.

We are not just here together to keep each other company. We are here together to show each other God. The portal is each other.

There are two forms of courage in this world. One demands that we jump into action with our armor on. The other demands that we strip ourselves bare-naked and surrender. Bravery is a curious thing.

Sometimes people walk away from love because it is so beautiful that it terrifies them. Sometimes they leave because the connection shines a bright light on their dark places and they are not ready to work them through. Sometimes they run away because they are not developmentally prepared to merge with another— they have more individuation work to do first. Sometimes they take off because love is not a priority in their lives—they have another path and purpose to walk first. Sometimes they end it because they prefer a relationship that is more practical than conscious, one that does not threaten the ways that they organize reality. Because so many of us carry shame, we have a tendency to personalize love's leavings, triggered by the rejection and feelings of abandonment. But this is not always true. Sometimes it has nothing to do with us. Sometimes the one who leaves is just not ready to hold it safe. Sometimes they know something we don't—they know their limits at that moment in time. Real love is no easy path—readiness is everything. May we grieve loss without personalizing it. May we learn to love ourselves in the absence of the lover.

The bones know.

I am tired of hearing what God is from head-tripping men. I am tired of hearing what God is from isolationists on a spiritual quest. I am tired of hearing what God is from lovers of detachment. I want to hear about a juicy God, a creative God, a relational God, a God that arises when we jump into life and stop playing it safe, watching it from afar like a passing train. It's time for the dancers to tell us what God is. It's time for the artists to tell us what God is. It's time for the lovers to tell us what God is. We are not here to watch God from afar. We are here to live God from the inside out.

One of the great challenges for those who have survived abusive or neglectful parents is that there is often a part of us that is still waiting for them to love us, even if there is very little chance of that happening. Locked in an archaic mindset, we continue to go back for more, looking for love in all the wrong places, still elevating them on a primal pedestal that does not even begin to reflect their human limitations and failings. Somehow we imagine that they will come around one day, realize their mistakes, see our worth, soften those armored edges. And some do, often when they are very old, made vulnerable by frailty and time. But many don't... and we need to stop putting our emotional lives on hold waiting for something that may never happen. The bridge from stagnation to empowerment lies in our willingness to see them for who they really are; to take them off their primal pedestal and recognize their human limitations. This is not easy—the hungry child-self clings to fantasies—but it is so very necessary. Until we accept the limitations of those who cannot love us, we cannot embrace the willingness of those who can.

The Buddha had a lot to offer around the detachment piece. Jesus had a lot to offer around the love piece. Jerry at the donut shop has a lot to offer around practicality. My friend Vanessa has a lot to offer around embodiment. Robin reminded us of the value of laughter. My favorite therapist really understands the value of a healthy self-concept. And on it goes. Lots of messengers everywhere, none of them fully realized, each offering a thread of wisdom. Without each other, just a bunch of random threads. Together, a sacred weave of wisdom. If there is such a thing as enlightenment, it does not exist within one person. It is a collective patchwork. The wholly holy.

Ecstasy and love are not the same thing. We often get them confused. There are some connections that open us so wide that we cannot help but call them love. But they may not be. They may just be a transcend-dance, an invitation to delight, the heart opening that we so desperately needed after years encased in armor. We call certain people into our lives to awaken us, to reheart us, but that doesn't mean they are the beloved. If a love is real, it is a portal to the everything, excavating light and shadow from their hiding places. The glory and the gory rise in unison, calling us to the sky and the earth in one fell swoop. Love is far more than floating to the heavens on a dreamy magic carpet. Love is sustainable. Love is inclusive. Love has feet that walk it through time.

As I get older, I recognize just how important it is to be surrounded by people who deeply believe in our value and goodness even when we lose our footing. It took me years to rid myself of the lite-dimmers and it has been much clearer sailing since. Not that there isn't value in having difficult people to overcome, but eventually it becomes essential to be surrounded by those who lift and wish us higher. If they don't see you in your highest light, wish them well and cut the cord.

My Dad used to say, "Your net worth is your gross realization." Now I understand his words.
Many people call 'accumulation' progress, while their inner world festers. When we actually heal and expand in consciousness, we stop caring about external accumulation. Progress becomes a process and not a tangible outcome. Then the real treasures are revealed.

The path of the spiritual warrior is not soft and sweet. It is not artificially blissful and feigned forgiving. It is not fearful of divisiveness. It is not afraid of its own shadow. It is not afraid of losing popularity when it speaks its truth. It will not beat around the bush where directness is essential. It has no regard for vested interests that cause suffering. It is benevolent and it is fiery and it is cuttingly honest in its efforts to liberate itself and humanity from the egoic ties that bind. Shunning strong opinions in the name of spirituality is anti-spiritual. Spirituality that is only floaty-soft is a recipe for disaster, allowing all manner of manipulation to run amok. Real spirituality is a quest for truth, in all its forms. Sometimes we find the truth on the meditation cushion, and sometimes we find it in the heart of legitimate conflict. May all spiritual warriors rise into fullness. This planet is lost without them.

(Dedicated to Andrew Harvey)

Many of us are shadow-jumpers. We jump away from life's difficulties with various techniques: self-distrActive behaviors, wishful thinking, feigned positivity, the spiritual bypass. With so little evidence that the shadow can be converted into light, we opt to float above our lives. And many of us are light-jumpers. We jump away from life's joys with various methods: perpetual pessimism, self-sabotage, emotional armor, the materialism bypass. With so little evidence that joy can be sustained, we avoid the possibility altogether. I call the healthy in-between 'Enrealment'—the capacity to hold both shadow and light at once, to live in all aspects of reality. Except in truly unbearable situations, we stay with the shadow until it transforms. And we enter the light when it beckons, strong enough to endure disappointment, open to the possibility that the light will grow stronger over time. Let's stop substituting avoidance for reality. We don't know how long we have—let's be here for all of it.

I look forward to the day when the only thing that ignites relationship
is two Souls calling out to one another,
two Soul-Hearts beating in the same direction, a
whisper of longing that bridges one essence to another.
I want to want you, not because it gratifies my ego, not
because you are outwardly beautiful,
but because your very presence invites my Godself out
of hiding.

We lose so many people every day to unresolved pain that overwhelms their consciousness. More than 800,000 people suicide each year worldwide—around one person every 40 seconds. Few are well-known. Most live anonymous lives. We must prioritize authentic revealing and emotional release in our world. We must slow down to see each other deeply and to share our inner worlds so that no one feels alone with their pain. We must find a way to bring our compassion to bare with others. There are so many of us here, yet so many suffer in isolation. We have to keep peeling the masks away. We have to keep sharing our truths. We have to. Our survival depends on it.

Let's give the masculine some real credit, particularly those armored men who are attempting to bust through traditional warrior structures. When a warrior man breaks through his armor and feels into his heart down below, this is a huge step forward for his consciousness and that of the collective. He has been conditioned to maintain a certain role on this planet and opening his heart is remarkably courageous. Many armored men are attempting this transition in modern life and it needs to be recognized. When they do, may we all understand how profound that is, and support them fully. Vigilance and vulnerability makes confusing bedfellows. Any man who is attempting to move from his receptivity is shattering long embedded paradigms. Deep bows to the tenderling warriors among us.

PUBLIC SERVICE ANNOUNCEMENT!

Due to the cumulative effect of collective sharing and loving intentionality, the Shame Train has derailed at the junction of Self-Belief and Divine Uniqueness. The engine couldn't run on self-hatred any longer. All formerly shamed passengers please disembark the train. You are free. A new train—fueled by healthy self-regard and sacred purpose—will be along momentarily to pick you up. No tickets required on this self-love train—just a growing faith in your own magnificence. All aboard!

When there has been too much pain, we often forget that we have the built-in capacity to move through it to another state. God gave us tears to be cried; God gave us the capacity to express our anger; God gave us a vast range of emotional devices that, when healthily unleashed and expressed, can clear the toxicity out of us, and lead us to lessons of self-love at the heart of them. In our authentic vulnerability lies our greatest power—the power to re-open our hearts after loss and disappointment. The idea that feeling the pain gives power to those who have hurt us is completely wrong. Feeling the pain is an act of self-empowerment and the only way to make a break from the prison of repressed emotions. Reach inside and unlock the door...

The polarities are changing with respect to gender. Soon it won't be men vs. women. It will be the awakening vs. the asleep, the heartfelt vs. the heartless, the selfless vs. the selfish. Men will rise up and stand beside women, in opposition to those men who imprison all of us. The kind of men who sexually assault women; the kind of men who manipulate economic systems solely for their own benefit; the kind of men who confuse aggression with assertiveness, will be met by a gender-inclusive force of benevolent souls, who will no longer tolerate the stripping of our human dignity, the raping of this planet or the women who mother it. I appreciate the good intentions of those who believe that we are ready to move away from opposition as a construct altogether, but I feel they are putting the heart before the force. It's premature. We still need to fight for our right to the light, and we need to do it together. Not as two polarized genders, but as souldiers of a higher order united by love, ready to march humanity into the light of compassion.

Love doesn't fail us—it's our expectations that fail us. Lovers sometimes forget that the gift is the call to love itself, and not the result. The quickening, the deepening, the merging, the burning bright in love's cosmic kiln. That's the great gift, no matter where it leads.

I no longer expect perfect offerings before I take someone into my heart. Nor do I ask myself to live up to an illusory standard of perfection before I accept myself. Because our humanness is not built on some objectively flawless foundation. Because we cannot grow as individuals if we are only moved by perfected action. We grow in increments, learning as we go, improving as we can. Perfectionism is incongruent with the natural pace of change. This is not to say that we should be satisfied with the lowest standard, but to acknowledge that we will not develop as individuals or as a species if we do not celebrate our little victories along the way. If we keep demanding perfection, we just perpetuate our collective shame. Better to pat ourselves, and others, on the back for every step forward, however humble it may be. We are not striving to become perfect. We are striving to become real, to show up for our life in every respect, flaws and all.

I was often a runner in relationship. I ran for all kinds of reasons. Sometimes it was a healthy flight: I wasn't ready to love, I had other priorities, I had preparation work to do before I could deeply connect. But sometimes I ran for unhealthy reasons—I imagined every woman my difficult mother, I associated family with trauma from my early life, I assumed love meant imprisonment. Distinguishing between healthy and unhealthy motivations took me many years, but it may have been the most important clarification work I did on my life's journey. Because if our flight from connection is motivated by our unresolved life history, our defenses can convince us to run for the rest of our lives. And then we lose the opportunity to taste a different reality, one that meets our needs and heals our hearts. It's worth examining: Am I running to something better, or am I running away from something unresolved? Am I retreating to heal, or am I simply delaying my liberation?

Love long and prosper.

New Cage Movement: A term to describe the more ungrounded, dangerous and simplistic elements of the New Age movement, including but not limited to: wishful thinking mantras, spiritual bypass and premature forgiveness practices, superficial healing techniques, the perpetual denial of common sense realities, and the insistence on inflated, fantastical perspectives—'Everything is an illusion,' 'It's all perfect,' 'There are no victims,' 'Anger is a sub-standard emotion,' 'Everything that happens is meant-to-be,' 'All judgments are bad,' 'You chose your every experience and circumstance,' 'Your personal identifications are inherently false,' 'Just ask the universe for what you want...,' 'Everything you see and feel is a reflection of you,' 'There is no one to blame,' 'The ego is the enemy,' etc. These perspectives have their place in certain circumstances, but taken too far—as they often are—become a prison of their own making, locking humanity in with its unresolved pain, obstructed from doing the real work by their addictive flights of fancy. On a relational level, New Cage connections are often woundmates, priding themselves in their seeming spirituality, but actually falling apart at the seams—unboundaried, ungrounded and controlled by all the unresolved emotional material that they have sought to avoid. In their determined efforts to float above the fray, they actually perpetuate and deepen their own suffering, and miss the opportunity to do the real work to become conscious together. The key to escaping New Cage prison is developing a willingness to do the real work to ground, embody and heal in authentic terms. There are no substitutes for genuine, hard-earned transformation.

The law of attraction is no 'secret' and it is profoundly misinterpreted. Sometimes we attract exactly what we need to grow, and sometimes a sociopath walks through the door, one who can fool anyone. Too many people stay in bad situations because they believe they have 'attracted' a necessary reflection. Sometimes this is true, but sometimes it is not. There is a reality to needless suffering, and misguided manifestation. We want to go where we grow, and not everything that comes into our life serves our expansion.

The measure of a healthy society is not how effectively it elevates its achievers, but how compassionately it supports those who have fallen.

You don't measure love in time. You measure love in transformation. Sometimes the longest connections yield very little growth, while the briefest of encounters change everything. The heart doesn't wear a watch—it's timeless. It doesn't care how long you know someone. It doesn't care if you had a 40-year anniversary if there is no juice in the connection. What the heart cares about is resonance. Resonance that opens it, resonance that enlivens it, resonance that calls it home. And when it finds it, the transformation begins...

The nature of awakening is not transcendence. It is not detachment. It is not leaving our bodies. It is not dismissing our shadow. It is not disparaging the ego. It is not feigned positivity. It is not bashing our story. It is not new age mysticism. The nature of awakening is inclusivity. It is connectiveness. It is shadow and light. It is enheartened presence. And presence is not to be found on the skyways of self-avoidance. Presence is to be found right down here, in our body temples, sole to soul on Mother Earth. Awakening requires that we show up for all of it. The great in-wakening.

It's not the sex act itself. It's the state we are in when we experience it. It's the heartfelt attention we bring to it. It's the intention that sources our longing. Some can have endless sex without being present for any of it. And some can have an occasional encounter and merge fully with God. Real intimacy requires real presence. And the remarkable thing about cultivating presence is that everything else becomes sacred. Everything becomes holy. You are always making love with the divine.

Sometimes people invite us into a drama that is of value to us—we have something to learn in the heart of it. But sometimes it is of no value to us—someone wants to live out their stuff, someone wants a wound-mate to join them in their trigger-fest. Drama loves company. Drama needs company to flourish. And if we grew up with chaos, we may jump in without realizing that boundaries were possible. Old drama habits die hard. We recreate what we know best. But we do have a choice. We really do. We can tell them to live it out somewhere else. We can establish a boundary. We can choose peace. Developing your 'no drama' muscle may well save your life. A drama-based lifestyle drains the adrenals and invites disease. It becomes a self-fulfilling prophecy that keeps coming back for more. Best to draw a line in the sand and refuse the invitation.

It's the heart that knows the path. The mind is just there to organize the steps.

I want to hear from the real people. Not the projected knowers. Not the vested interests. Not the Hollywood spiritualists. I want to hear from the ones who have to find the light in a challenging daily life. The ones who have to overcome the odds to find the faith. The ones who choose to hold to their truths when falsity will pay the bills. I want to hear from the real ones.

We're all sensitive. Some of us just hide it better.

It can be so difficult when someone we are in relationship with decides that they need to separate in order to find themselves. This is not to be taken personally. Some can clarify who they are while in the heart of relationship, but not everyone can. Some really do need to separate in order to find their individual identity. They need the space to explore, to clarify, to integrate their realizations. They simply aren't ready to deal with another person's energy and issues. As long as it's not an avoidant flight from intimacy, this can be a very positive decision. Individuation is an essential step on the road to a sustainable relationship. If they are not at peace with their individual path, they will not be healthy, attuned partners. At the same time, one should not put their life on hold waiting for them. The fact is, they may never return, and, even if they do, you have no way of knowing who they will be then. You fell in love with who they were at a moment in time—but that moment has passed. They are uncovering a new identity now. Extend that offering to yourself as well. Move on from them and see where the river takes you, too.

I know we often want it happy and positive, but that's just not where much of humanity is. Many of us are overwhelmed with pain, undigested sadness, unexpressed anger, unseen truths. This is where we are at, as a collective. So we have two choices. We can continue to pretend it's not there, cover it over, shame and shun it in ourselves and others, distract and detach whenever possible. Or, we can face it heart-on, own it within ourselves, look for it in others with compassion, create a culture that is focused on authenticity and healthy emotional release. If we continue to push it all down, we are both creating illness, and delaying our collective expansion. But if we can just own the shadow, express it, release it, love each other through it—we can finally graduate from the School of Heart Knocks and begin to enjoy this magnificent life as we were intended. Pretending the pain isn't there just embeds it further. Let's illuminate it instead.

It can be so subtle, can't it? The ways we avoid the real. I still catch myself using positivity and perfection as a cover, as a way of avoiding those confusing, chaotic and disappointing places that feel uncomfortable. Yes, there is a place for order and achievement, but if we can't live in the discomforts, we aren't really here. We can't be here and only show up for some of it, can we? It's all divinity, even the murky, the mucky, the mad. How can it be any other way? To be human is to touch it all.

Real closeness is not hiding co-dependently in another's presence. Real closeness is not getting so lost in another that you no longer exist as a separate entity. Real closeness is two sovereign beings far enough back from each other to see a separate other, yet close enough to bridge their hearts. Two interconnected soulitudes.

I am so tired of people saying, "You are exactly where you are supposed to be," no matter what someone's life circumstances and challenges. Yes, there is no question that we can often learn something of value wherever we are on the path; and yes, we may have, in some situations, attracted the exact challenge that we need to grow, BUT that does not mean that we are ALWAYS where we are supposed to be, or that we chose our reality. Telling that to someone in every situation—even when they are ill or suffering tremendously—is arrogant, and adds insult to injury. Sometimes we need a kick in the ass, and sometimes we are just a victim of terrible circumstances. Sometimes we chose our reality, and sometimes it just chose us. Sometimes our suffering is needless and the result of other people's wrongdoing. Compassion demands that we hold the space for other's challenges with a wide open heart. Let them decide if they are exactly where they are supposed to be. It's not for us to say.

Clearing our emotional debris has many positive consequences with respect to love connection. It creates more space inside for love to enter, and it gives us more energy to see love through. Unresolved material is like undigested food—it blocks the channel and prevents new nourishment from entering. All bunked up, we may not even notice love when it walks through the door. Releasing our emotional holdings cleans our lens, allowing us to notice love when it comes. And working through our issues expands our awarenest, providing us with the tools we will need to manage our triggers and patterns when they arise. Of course, love will excavate unseen issues from their hiding places, but with more awareness of the processes of pattern recognition and healing, we stand a better chance of staying out of our own way. If you aren't familiar with the stuff you came in with, you are going to have a hard time managing the new levels of material that the love excavates. This is the actual new earth. Not a place where we sit around staring at our wounds like self-avoidant automatons, but one where we actually do the work to heal and grow through our unresolved material. So that we can truly show up when love comes.

Dear UNconscious members of the media: Please take some time off. Seriously—you must need a vacation. Rest, remember yourself. It takes a lot of energy to exaggerate reality, to darken the sky, to shove tragedy in the faces of humanity until we are overcome with so much survivalist anxiety that we are gripped to your news reports. Surely you must be exhausted from playing this nasty little game that leaves people nervous and frightened, often without cause. Surely we don't need to know the gruesome details of yet another shooting. Surely you don't feel good about being pawns in a system that makes money from making people depressed and afraid. Surely your ultimate calling in life is not to be a merchant of doom, commodifying our anxiety and converting it into dollars. When I look outside, I see the sun shining. I see a woman walking her dog. I see a car passing by. I don't see tragedy everywhere I look. Why do you?

When I would go to bed with a woman when I was young, I didn't realize that there were many of us in the bed at the same time. There was her and I, her parents, my parents, our past lovers, and anyone else we had unfinished business with. That's the thing about being unconscious—we can't help but bring our unresolved baggage into every relational encounter. Talk about an unwelcome orgy! It's a busy bed when we are unconscious. A little hard to move around freely with so many projections on the mattress. One of the reasons we do the work to heal our past is so that we can actually create more space for intimacy. With our patterns fallen away, we stand a much better chance of holding love safe. With our projections worked through, we can actually see the beloved with clear eyes. Finally, it's just the two of us...

Anger is a river. It wants to be released into the vaster ocean. It wants to move naturally. When we repress it with premature forgiveness, block it with false positivity, suppress it in the name of pseudo-peace, we dam(n) our natural flow. The river then turns inward, against the self; or explodes outwardly, against innocents. Better we express it when it arises—not in a way that is destructive to humanity—but in a way that is authentic and that restores the integrity of our being. Anger isn't the enemy. Misplaced anger is. Let the river flow...

It took me years to understand the impact of being a scapegoat in my childhood home. To survive it, I armored up, muscling my way across the family battleground to safety. But safety didn't mean that the patterns subsided. In fact, the internalized remnants of being 'the one to blame' became even more evident later in life. Being the scapegoat was manifest in many intertwined tendencies: self-shaming, self-hatred, feeling unwelcome in my own body, vicarious justice-seeking, feeling responsible for things that happened to those I knew ('I should have saved them') and sometimes, even for things that happened to strangers. Being blamed for the lives of others is a tremendous burden, difficult to shed. If you carry this weight, devote real time to looking at how it interferes with your daily life, your faith in yourself, the choices you make. Call out those who blamed you in the past—no child can be responsible for an adult's misery—and boundary those who continue to scapegoat you. We are all entitled to feel worthy of our time here.

The quest for enlightenment bores me. It bores me and distracts me from the real work required to truly grow. It's so up there, and my challenges are so down here. The karmic field for my soul's expansion is in the heart of my imperfect patterns. It's in the transforming fires of daily experience. It's in the heat of my real life—not the transcendent life, not the detached life, not the projected perfect life—but right here, in this blessed and aging body temple. It's all I can do to embody my humanness—I have no time to waste striving to rise above it. The imperfect quest for an authentic life is perfect enough for me.

As I look back at all the places I have loved from—energetic harmony, sexual electricity, intellectual alignment—I am certain that none of them could sustain love over a lifetime. The only thing I have ever found that could is a genuine fascination with a woman's inner world, with the way she organizes reality, with the unfathomable mysteries of her essence. To hear her soul cry out to me again and again, and to never lose interest in what it is trying to convey. If there is that, then there will be still be love when the body falls apart, when the perfection projection is shattered, when the sexual charge dissipates. If there is that, you will swim in love's waters until the very last breath.

In order to deal with the feelings related to the absent or abusive parent, children often make the assumption that they are to blame. This is the only way they can make sense of it—if the adult isn't loving, it must be because we are 'unworthy.' Thus begins the internalized shame and self-blame cycle, often reflected in the disdain we feel for our bodies, our creations, our very existence. This cycle is often perpetuated and deepened by spiritual bypass communities who diminish the seekers daring to work on their unresolved feelings, by telling them that their feelings are an illusion, their experiences are mischaracterized, their stories tiresome. Let's get this straight—shame is not an illusion. Self-loathing is not an illusion. Abuse is not an illusion. And the need to heal our hearts and elevate our self-concepts is essential to healthy functioning. Pretending things aren't real doesn't make them go away. Facing them does.

I am not another you. You are not another me. Let's not wash away our uniqueness in the ocean of all-Oneness. Yes, we are connected. Yes, we are all part of the oneness. Yes, we all experience similar challenges and delights. But we are not the same. Each of us is unique. Each of us has distinct callings and gifts. Each of us is here with a very specific sacred purpose. The idea that we are 'All-One' takes on a whole new meaning when we interact with unity from an individuated and clarified purpose. There is the ocean of essence, and there is the individual droplet of meaning. Every soul has a unique role to play in this dance of sacred imagination.

I sit at a coffee shop watching the world go by. Dozens of cars lined up for yet another coffee. Two kids arguing over I-pad time. Deep fried heart-stoppers called donuts eaten in abundance. Me spending much too much time worrying and on the computer. Cirque du soul-eh? The sanest one is the little poodle outside, who is barking to his heart's content, not distracting, not worrying about things that don't matter—just living. Now if only we could all just realeyes how funny it all is and go hang with the poodle. My new spiritual teacher...

Let's get real about the ole, 'What we judge in others is a direct reflection of what exists within ourselves' routine. To be sure, there is value in considering how we are projecting our own stuff onto others—that is a wise inquiry—but let's not throw discernment out with the bathwater. Not every negative judgment we feel is sourced in our own stuff, or in a past life projection trail. Sometimes our judgments are actually reflections of a conscious discernment process. Sometimes we are appalled by certain behaviors because we have evolved to the point where we can distinguish good from bad, healthy from unhealthy, benevolent from malevolent. Do you know who perpetuated the anti-judgment mantra with the world? Gurus who wanted to deflect responsibility when they were not living up to their professed standards. You call them on their stuff and they turn the mirror right back on you. It all comes back to good ole common sense. Sometimes we are projecting, and sometimes we are seeing things exactly as they are. Enrealment or EnBullshitment—pick your path.

Love meets in many places—some form, others formless. I have tried both meeting points. Like many conditioned men, I began my intimacy journey with form—fleshy, juicy, tangible form, often confusing lust with love, orgasm with ourgasm, intensity with divinity. But that got boring fast. And then I swung to the formless, the mystical, the transcendent, the kind of love that meets in the subtleties, within the bliss. But that became unreal, with no form to embody it. I found my peace on the bridge between the two, in an integration of form and formless, at that point of contact where mysticism meets embodiment meets God. What is love without form? And what is form without love?

It is always good to remember that we have all the healing tools we need inside of us. For every wound, there is a healing path. That is not to say that we don't need support, but if we can just give ourselves permission to move the darkness out, more light will come in to fill the empty space. We can do a thousand workshops and read another thousand books, but if we don't make the courageous decision to let go of what we carry, we won't grow an inch.

There is a meaningful difference between default positivity and conscious positivity. Default positivity is when we turn to positivity as a mechanism, an adaptation, a defense against owning or feeling the shadow. Often birthed in challenging life experiences, this pseudo-bliss trip can keep us alive during tumultuous times, but it can also become an embedded way of being that detaches us from our authenticity. Conscious positivity is birthed in awareness and authenticity. We don't default to positive thinking in an effort to avoid discomfort—we turn to it when it feels organic and true in the moment. Smiling from the core outward...

It is one of life's greatest challenges to go from intimacy with the beloved to intimacy with a mere mortal. Of course, the beloved is surely mortal, but the contrast between soul-sourced intimacy and attraction-driven intimacy can be startling after you have touched God with love's fingers. The sexual body has become indistinguishable from the divine and longs to remain united. Separating them again feels like a kind of suicide, a desecration of one's innermost holiness. Better to have the memory of one beloved, than the presence of a thousand sexy imposters.

My mother believed that she should stay in her difficult marriage with my father for the sake of the kids. Was she ever wrong. In fact, their miserable marriage became a prison of gloom for her children, one that offered no glimmer of hope, one that modeled misery and frustration as a way of being. When they were together, I was failing high school and unable to find the light in the darkness. After they split up, I began to excel at school and opened my first student business—my life made a turn for the better. Neither path was easy, but the end of the gloom-fest opened up doors where before there was no exit. Not to pretend for one moment that changing a family structure is easy, particularly when there are financial challenges, but it's not always as hopeless as it seems...

I make a distinction between standards and expectations with respect to relationships. Expectations only serve to hamper us, unless what we are expecting is something that someone has agreed to give. If they haven't, then our expectations will only impede the possibility of genuine connection. But standards—for example, to be met with a certain degree of kindness and attunement—serve us well in all forms of relationship, ensuring that we do not forget how we wish to be related to. When we drop our expectations, possibilities open up. When we drop our standards, trouble often follows.

Don't be concerned about what people say about your life choices. It is all any of us can do to clarify our own steps—we cannot possibly know another's. And besides, lots of people had their wisdom truths removed at an early age. They just like to hear themselves talk. Don't listen. You are the sculptor of your own reality—don't hand your tools to anyone else.

Aging has its benefits with respect to the quest for the right partner. Less time to come creates a more focused lens. Where there was once all kinds of time to delay intimacy, now there is just enough time to give love a shot. I spent a lot of years wasting precious time on inappropriate connections. I had things to learn, to be sure, but too much time was spent clinging to the illusion of security at the expense of my soul's longing. Aging can help with that. Nothing like a view of the end to spark our hearts into action.

Dear unconscious men,

Stop dissing women. Stop harassing women. Stop buying women. Stop hitting women. Stop hunting women. Stop kidnapping women. Stop raping women. Start respecting women. Start honoring women. Start protecting women. Start nurturing women. Start comforting women. Start celebrating women. Start loving women.

So much of my inner work in this lifetime has revolved around trying to find the middle—that place between self-elevation and self-diminishment where real life happens. Perhaps you can relate. I grew up internalizing two conflicting and untrue messages in my family of origin. The first, that of the devil child who is to blame for the family's suffering. The second, that of the great savior who will raise the family from the ashes of despair. As a result, I spent many years swinging back and forth between self-hatred and self-aggrandizement, neither of which are amenable to healthy functioning. The work for anyone with this pattern is to learn how to love themselves just as they are. Not perfect and not horrible, but simply and beautifully human.

So called 'late-bloomers' get a bad rap. Sometimes the people with the greatest potential often take the longest to find their path because their sensitivity is a double-edged sword—it lives at the heart of their brilliance, but it also makes them more susceptible to life's pains. Good thing we aren't penalized for handing in our purpose late. The soul doesn't know a thing about deadlines.

I am always surprised when friends apologize for being in a bad mood, or sharing their life challenges when I bump into them, as though there is something wrong with sharing our difficulties with each other. This is yet another example of the bullshit positivity world we have created in Western life, where we are only acceptable to each other if we share good news. I often wonder if we are resistant to other's bad news because we are trying to bypass our own difficulties. Whatever it is, this has to shift. We aren't going to co-create a genuinely positive world until we can hold the space for each other's shadow. Better an authentic frown than an inauthentic smile any day. A smile that is built on a pretentious foundation isn't a smile at all.

There is often someone running away from a beautiful love connection, but it's seldom the brave one. The brave one is usually the one left behind. It seems counter-intuitive to romantics and those who feel ready to partner when someone walks away. But some people can only handle a half-love because a whole love shines a light on their dark places. Real intimacy requires real presence. If someone isn't ready to be truly here on an individual level, they will find it very difficult to manage all the triggers that come up in connection. Only a small few can hold the gate open when profound love enters. A blessed and courageous few.

It's not "all an illusion." Let's be clear about that. Sometimes our interpretation is an illusion, sometimes the presentation is an illusion, sometimes our identifications are premised on an illusory foundation, but it's seldom ALL an illusion. Countless gurus and spiritual teachers have used "It's all an illusion" in an effort to bypass responsibility for their misdeeds. It's all reality when it serves them, and it's all an illusion when it doesn't. We have to be careful with this kind of languaging. Healthily applied, "it's all an illusion" supports a conscious inquiry into what is real and what isn't. Unhealthily applied, it supports the manipulation of humanity. Sometimes it's an illusion, sometimes it isn't. And it's for each individual to discern the difference on their own terms.

Playing small serves no one. It's a consequence of a shaming culture, one that has not been ready to embrace our individual magnificence. It seems everyone I know—-myself included—struggles with the challenge of embodying their wholeness, as though it's a crime to be a wondrous, amazing, self-loving being. And the ungrounded spiritual community has contributed to this confusion by desacralizing the ego in its entirety, rather than making the intelligent distinction between the healthy and unhealthy ego. Seekers end up lost in the middle—reluctant to imagine themselves magnificent—and, at the same time, immobilized by a negative self-concept. The answer is to support each other in actualizing all that we are—not in a way that contributes to a narcissistic self-concept—but in a way that supports our movement toward wholeness. We have so many gifts inside, a treasure trove of wonder just waiting to be lived...

The primary cause of our unhappiness is not our thoughts. It is our undigested emotional material. Forget the monkey mind. Shifting out of unhappiness is not a cerebral process—that's just another ineffective band-aid—it is a felt experience. It's the monkey heart that's the issue—the state of inner tumult and chaos that emanates from an unclear heart. Flooded with unresolved emotions and unexpressed truths, the monkey heart jumps from tree-top to tree-top, emoting without grounding, dancing in its confusion. Often misinterpreted as a monkey mind, the monkey heart is reflected in unsettled, repetitive thinking. To calm and clarify it, one may benefit from heartfulness practices: emotional release, armor-busters, depth charges, heart openers. If you want to change your thinking, heal your heart. That's the best meditation of all.

I remember how determinedly I would cover over my need for comfort with sexual activity. It was easier to get excited and go for it, then to drop into my heart and admit that what I really needed was to be comforted. As a conditioned male warrior, the last thing I wanted was to appear fragile and worn. I had to remain vigilant, intense, passionate. No vulnerability allowed. And as I look out at the world we live in, I see the imprints of this covering over everywhere. We are such an under-comforted world; masking our need to be seen, held and valued, below all manner of distraction and disguise. As we continue on our quest for a truer life, I invite all of us to connect with the comforting we need. Not to deny it, not to distort it—but to own it, to ask for it, to provide it for ourselves if no one else will. Imagine the world where everyone has comfort in the storms of life. That's the kind of intimacy that heals.

Sensitivity is divinity.

The best thing about haters is that they help us to heal our childhood wounds. Every time they come our way, we get another opportunity to love ourselves in the heart of their contempt. Where before attack and criticism triggered us into hiding, we now hear ourselves ROAR! with readiness. You can't bring your voice to the world without triggering others. You can't find your light without pissing someone off. It comes with the territory. So, ROAR in the face of the light-dimmers. ROAR!!!

There is this moment, after a beloved has left, when you have a choice to make. Do you close your heart to life, or do you feed the fires of deep feeling? Do you get lost in your memories, or convert them into new possibilities? Do you go blind to love, or do you see it everywhere? It helps to realize that love is always a blessed visitor. We have no guarantee it will come our way. Even a moment of it is a great gift from Providence. Better we build on our blessings.

If it's ALL a mirror, then I got me some work to do. No wait, no need—it's ALL an illusion. :) Wait, how can it be both? If it's all an illusion, there isn't anything to mirror. And if it's all a mirror, then none of it is an illusion. Methinks the New Cage movement is confusing its bypass mantras! My illusory head just smashed my illusory mirror into illusory bits. Watch where you step, or not.

I believe in unconditional love, but I don't believe in unconditional relationships. There must always be a condition of kindness.

It doesn't change when we stare at it from across the room. It doesn't change when we sit in prayer and wish it away. It doesn't change when we skirt the edges of the shadow. It doesn't change when we pretend it's all Go(o)d. It changes when we cross the sacred battleground willing to die to our truth. It changes when we look the lie in the eye until it has nowhere left to hide. It changes when we pick up the sword of truth and cut the falsity until it bleeds right through. The era of the sacred activist is upon us. Not the warrior run amok, but the benevolent warrior who fights for our right to the light. Some battles are worth fighting.

I distinguish between those situations where there is still work to be done in a relationship, and those where the work has come to an end. All too often, we remain locked into connections that no longer serve us. And, all too often, we let go of connections before our work together is complete. We have to decide—is this relationship a laboratory for my own expansion, or a prison of my own making? Does it invite growth, or induce sleep? Can we find a way to become conscious together, or are we better off apart? This is the (he)art form of relatedness—knowing when to dive in deeper, knowing when to step away. Once we perfect this art, we can grow forward in our relational life.

If one claims to be a 'realized master' then they are, by definition, not. For anyone who grows in awareness realizes that there is so much more left unseen, so many wisdoms yet unknown, a million learnings to come. In my experience, those who claim to be realized masters are usually grifters in guru garb, and, in fact, remarkably unsure of their own value. Their claim of life mastery is an over-compensatory, egoic claim that masks a profound insecurity. It is not to be taken seriously. Better we sit with those who both recognize their offerings and honor their limitations.

Detachment is a tool—it's not a life.

I heard it all from my parental wardens in early life: "You are stupid. You are to blame. It was better before you came along. You are unworthy. You are a crying shame." And a little voice inside my little body told me that it was their stuff. And it was—it was never mine. Whatever belittling messages you are presently subject to, don't believe them. They are a reflection of the communicator's inner world, and say nothing about you. Because your inherent value is not determined by other humans. It was already granted to you by Providence. You were born with worthiness at the heart of every breath.

The body is the heart of the matter, the soul's garden of truth. If we don't take care of the body-temple, there will be no place to pray.

The Silent Routine. Do you know that one? I know it well. When I was a kid, I ran towards people who used silence as a way to torment. They were my parents, after all. A kid needs their attention and attunement to develop. This pattern plagued me for many years, despite reaching the stage where I cognitively understood what was happening. It was a deep and familiar groove, after all. Over time, I have worked this through. I now say goodbye to those who passively use silence as a form of expression. They have no place in my life. What helped me to reach this stage was working the self-concept piece. With a healthier sense of self, I have no resonance with anything that does not reflect it. The more deeply we value ourselves, the easier it gets to say farewell to those who do not.

I understand that we get lost in our stories, but let's not throw out the whole story with the bathwater. In the heart of our story is the grist for our soul's transformation. Our stories are no illusion. We are made of story. The illusion is illusion, itself. Deal with your story, or your story will deal with you.

Emotional armor is not easy to shed, nor should it be. It has formed for a reason: as a requirement for certain responsibilities, as a conditioned response to real circumstances, as a defense against unbearable feelings. It has served an essential purpose. It has saved lives. Yet it can be softened over time. It can melt into the tendernest at its core. It can reveal the light at its source. But never rush it, never push up against it, never demand it to drop its guard before its time. Because it knows something you don't. In a still frightening world, armor is no less valid than vulnerability. Let it shed at its own unique pace.

Perhaps the most important question you can ask a potential love partner relates to their relationship with the shadow—their own, and the shadow that emerges in the relationship itself. That is, "How much work are you willing to do on yourself and the relationship when the s* # t hits the fan? Are you willing to go as deep as we have to go to work it through, or are you only interested in a breezy, low-maintenance relationship?" Few people ever talk about this during the romantic phase, because they are not envisioning the challenges to come. Yet it is an essential inquiry. I have known many people who were shocked to watch their 'great love' walk out the door when the connection required personal accountability and therapeutic work-through. Some of us will brave the journey; others will flee the fire. Some of us will do the work to transform our stories into the light at their source; others will run away with their 'tales' between their legs, only to find out later that their tales go with them everywhere they go. If we can determine someone's willingness at the beginning, we can save ourselves a lot of trouble later.

The veil is thin between being blind to each other and seeing ourselves in each other. We walk past each other on the street, we sit beside each other in our separate vehicles, yet we don't realize how similar we are below our masks and adaptations. Our paths are similar, our worries are similar, our longings are similar. In the next stage of collective expansion, we must get below the disguises that blind us to each other. We must realeyes that we are in this together. I want to see you, I want to be seen, I want to share the truth of this odd and fantastic life trip with my fellow humans. The authentic truth—not the cloaked version that we have been conditioned to present. So much changes when we recognize that we are walking to the same soul-beat on the trailways of transformation. So much.

If you meet the Buddha on the road, kiss him. Give him a taste of healthy desire that he won't soon forget.

Those who don't want to deal with their issues have a tendency to pass them onto someone else. Then they can pretend they don't have them anymore. Unfortunately, some of us become carriers of the virus—carrying another's unresolved toxicity up the hill, legs buckling, short of breath, close to collapse. It's too much. It's hard enough to get through life without adding someone else's stuff to our load. It is essential that we do a conscious baggage check now and then, being painstakingly honest with ourselves about the ways that we have accumulated other people's stuff: What form is it in? How heavy is it? How does it block our expansion? Whose baggage is this, anyway? No one, absolutely no one, has the right to pass their stuff to another without their permission. If you have someone's baggage in tow—check it at the nearest dump. It's only yours if you choose to carry it. Better to travel life's highways light.

All too often, parents hold themselves back from pursuing their individual dreams because they have responsibilities to their children. They don't want their children to feel neglected and abandoned. But often there is a way to remain devoted, while still actualizing one's own callings. My parents both sacrificed elements of their own paths for their children. I am not sure it helped anyone. They ended up bitter and regretful, and denied their children two essential things: an opportunity to see self-realization modeled to us; and the confidence-building that comes from being inextricably linked to an actualized legacy. Yes, there can be something beautiful about sacrificing our individual path for others... but seeing a parent become all that they are meant to become may well give the kids the boost they need to believe in their own possibilities.

If all you have is a loveship, you are unlikely to survive troubled waters. With no ability to work together to overcome love's challenges, it will be very difficult to remain afloat. At some point on the journey, your ship is going to capsize. What is love without relatedness? If all you have is a relationship, then you may well remain afloat, but there will be a longing for something more, a love that sets your soul ablaze. What is relatedness without love? But if you have a loveship AND a relationship, there is no limit to how far your bond can travel on the oceans of essence. Love that is grounded in healthy relatedness is like a buffer against the madness of the world. The more difficult the challenges, the stronger the bond grows. The bigger the soulnami, the sturdier the foundation that meets it.

It's an odd thing how willing we are to see divinity in others, but not in ourselves. This one is enlightened, that one is cool, the other one is brilliant, but what about the beautiful being staring at us in the mirror? Chopped liver? Sub-standard? A big mistake? Seems kind of crazy, doesn't it! I somehow imagine that this world will not become a better place until we see God in our own two eyes. There he is, looking right back at us, loving her creation. And then, through our God-eyes, we can see others for who they are. Not as projected figures of light, but as fellow beams of wholeness, perfectly imperfect threads of the eternal God weave. We're all reflections of the creator, every last one of us.

I make a distinction between relationship challenges that are sourced in trauma and those sourced in developmental stages. Quite often, they are inextricably linked, but not always. Sometimes what is blocking someone's emotional availability and fueling dysfunctional behavior is primarily related to unhealed traumas. But sometimes the deeper issue is that they are at a different emotional stage. In the latter case, it is not simply a question of holding the space for their healing. It's a question of waiting, often for years, in the hope that they reach the stage you are at. An impossible scenario, both because you will have to stop growing yourself if they are to catch up, and because you really don't know who they will be at the next stages of their developmental journey. They may grow into someone perfectly compatible with you, or they may move in another direction altogether. Perhaps the most important questions we can ask about a partner relates to their emotional age: How emotionally mature are they? What areas have they developed and integrated? What aspects are still under-developed? And how will their stage of development intersect with ours? Don't be fooled by chronological age. Stage—not age—is what matters most.

Truth-aches come in many forms, in their earnest efforts to call us home: perpetual dissatisfaction, a nudging sense of falsity, a little voice that wakes us up at night demanding change. I often imagine myself with two primary currents running through my veins—the oceans of essence that reflect my sacred purpose, and the dam(n)ed up river that reflects my misidentifications. Where to swim in this life? Swim True.

There's not always a lesson related to who we chose. Sometimes we chose for all the right reasons, and still got fooled. Sometimes the lesson comes later, when we have to decide whether to close our hearts, or give love another try. If we can learn how to re-open our hearts despite our disappointments, then we have learned well. There is no better way to assert our value than refusing to give up on our right to love and be loved.

We must not give up. It takes so much time to heal because we are not just healing our own wounds—we are healing the world's wounds, too. We think we are alone with our 'stuff', but we aren't. With every clearing of our emotional debris, with every foray into a healthier way of being, with every excavation and release of old material, we heal the collective heart. So many of our familial and karmic ancestors had little opportunity to heal their pains. When we heal, their spirits breathe a sigh of relief. We heal them backwards, while healing ourselves forward. We heal in unison.

I know some couples who actually enjoy triggering each other. They enjoy it because they believe that they need the triggers in order to bring their unresolved wounds and patterns to the surface. For them, their tumultuous connection is the primary way they become conscious of their issues. This is one kind of conscious relationship, although one has to be careful to distinguish forward moving trigger-fests from co-dependent wound-mating. I prefer another kind— one where the connection is so stable and kind that your armor melts into sweetness. In the heart of that opening, your wounds and issues feel safe to reveal themselves. Not perpetually triggered by your partner, not re-traumatized by the connection, but invited into awareness and healing by their loving presence. That's my kind of conscious relationship. To each their path home.

Perhaps if we stop looking for love,
we will realize that it is breathing us.

Much of human history has been plagued by a collective fear of revealing our truths to each other. Mistakes we may have made, seeming imperfections and family secrets all got buried beneath a motherload of shame. And, of course, other shamed individuals perpetuated this pattern by publicly shaming us as they had been shamed. And what a shame that is, for we will not heal and evolve as a species until we stop hiding our truths from each other. Self-revealing frees us from the shaming ties that bind and gives others the permission they need to reveal themselves as well. This is the place to work, as a collective, to restore our sense of our own worth, to learn how to validate others, to co-create a celebratory way of being that recognizes the fact that we are all here because we are welcome here. Our humanness is not something we have to cloak and bury. The reveal is for real.

It's very hard to be objective about relationships that are inextricably woven into the breath of your being, indistinguishable from your waking consciousness. Some call these connections co-dependent, but it's not always like that. Sometimes there is a mystical pull between two souls that transcends psychological factors. Sometimes a connection is a divine imperative, God calling out to God in fleshy form. When two destined hearts beat in the same direction, all gaps narrow. That's not co-dependency—that's co-creation.

Dear Divine Feminine,

My awakening brothers and I are continuing our movement into the heart as a way of being. It's a slow-winged process, but we are dropping down a little more with every lesson. Bless us with your ongoing support as we figure out how to not figure it out, and, to simply feel our way home. We have some experience with the relational path, but not as much as you do. We have often moved with a heartfelt intention, but swimming in deep feeling is another experience entirely. We have been so vigilant for so long that it's a challenge to relate to the moment vulnerably. We do intuit that the life of the heart is the path home, but we need some time to embrace it, to integrate it, to understand how to move the way that loves makes you move. We have the willingness—we just have to learn how to convert our armored nature into receptivity. We have for too long associated surrender with weakness. But it is not. It is the depths of courage. You have taught us that. Please be patient as we stumble back to our old patterns. Once we understand this new way, we will not disappoint you. We will meet you there.

Authenticity is not just a word. It's not just a trendy concept. It's not just a way to sell product. It's a heartcore path. It's a perilous path. It's a way of being that is not influenced by political considerations, not concerned with how it will be judged, not souling itself out for the mighty dollar. An authentic being bows down before nothing untrue. (S)he owns her truth no matter the consequences. (S)he is inspired from the inside out. It's time to reclaim the word 'authentic,' before it becomes as disingenuous as the words 'enlightened' and 'spiritual'. It ain't authentic unless it's nakedly true.

We have a natural tendency to assume that a remarkable chemistry between two souls is confirmation that they are meant to be together for life. In the heat of profound feelings, it seems counter-intuitive to imagine ourselves separate from a beloved. But chemistry and longevity are not necessarily bedfellows. Just because we feel earth-shatteringly alive with someone doesn't mean they are supposed to be our life partner. They may have come for a very different reason—to awaken us, to expand us, to shatter us so wide open that we can never close again. Perhaps they were sent from afar to polish the rough diamond of your soul before vanishing into eternity. Perhaps they just came to give us new eyes. Better we surrender our expectations when a beloved comes. (S)he may just be dropping in for a visit. Is the kettle on?

It's difficult to let go of the pattern—often born in our childhood tendency to try to get love from a stone (neglectful parents)—to be attracted to those who are impossible. It's like only the emotionally unavailable are credible because they reflect back to us what we came to believe about ourselves—that we are unworthy of love—and it's an odd illusion that if we can get the inaccessible to love us that we will finally have our parents love. The more obvious approach— that we share love with someone who can truly give it—often gets lost in the karmic shuffle. This pattern is not an easy one to break, but break-through it we must if we are going to finally surrender to the love we deserve. One of the keys to working this through is to see the parents for who they really are—in their own issues and limitations—so that their lens on you loses its grip. Another is building the self-concept from the inside out—learning to rely on yourself for validation—and, when you are ready, inviting those who value you a little closer...

Often when I achieve something that means something to me, I am met with jealousy. Not from many, but always from a few. The jealousy is often shrouded in some other languaging, but I can spot jealousy from a mile away. I had jealous parents, after all. What the jealous don't realize is that their jealousy says more about them than it does about me. Their jealousy is a lighthouse that points to what is frustratingly unactualized within them. It is a perfect opportunity to own their own dissatisfaction with their path. It is an invitation to both see and work through their own obstructions to humanifestation. Don't waste time being jealous of another's creations. Get on with the business of finding and living your own sacred purpose. When you do, you will be delighted when others do the same.

Yet another tenet of the ungrounded spirituality movement is to blame people for their physical illnesses. If only they had dealt with their past life issues, if only they had become more aware, if only they had processed more of their emotional pain, if only... Not only are these comments presumptuous—only the person with the illness can make those statements—but they ignore the very simple fact that illness is often sourced in many factors, a number of which are not easily identifiable and certainly not attributable to karma or awareness or emotional health. Sometimes people just get sick. I have seen too many new cagers working someone else's illness as an egoic boost, narcissistically using it as evidence of their own superiority: "Well, I didn't get sick, because I am a more evolved person." Nonsense! If you are more evolved, you will move from compassion and humility. Sometimes people just get sick, and if you can't respond empathically, keep quiet. Let them decipher where their illness comes from. They don't need insult added to injury. They need our presence.

If someone really loves you, they love you just as you are. Their love is not dependent on whether you get a tummy tuck, wear their favorite outfit, do a perfect downward dog. Their love is not conditional on whether you meet their every need, their every whim, their every fantasy. Their love is not contingent on you changing your lifestyle or transforming your personality. If they really love you, they hold you in the highest light. If they really love you, they are too busy giving to you to notice petty details. If they really love you, they see divinity when they look your way. And the divine is not in need of improvement before s(he) is loved!

There really is no feeling like re-connecting with a soul that you have known since time immemorial. Not only does it bridge you to each other, but it grounds you deeper into your own karmic legacy. Suddenly the worries of the day aren't quite as pressing, as the cozy blanket of shared lineage holds you safe, reminding you that you have both been here before and that you will surely be here again. In the eyes of the beloved is the evidence that life truly goes on. You meet in the deep within, again and again. Soulmates both call us back in time and prepare the nest for our lives to come.

If I just do another workshop, if I just meditate a few more hours, if I just do more downward dogs, if I just do more hours of tantra, if I just read more spiritual texts, if I just attend more kirtans, if I just pray to more altars, if I just buy more crystals, if I just do more cleanses, if I just eat more live food, if I just serve more gurus, if I just have more a-ha moments, if I just do more ayahuasca, if I just... I will become more enlightened. Yes, some activities do support our expansion, but how about just going for a walk and breathing? Got as good a chance of being here now with your souls making contact with Mother Earth than anywhere else. Be real now—how's that for a no-plan?

Real change is seldom a giant step. It is usually a small one. Small but deeply real. We hold the fear and the faith at the same time... and we cross the bridge slowly. When we get to the other side, we have been transformed—not by the step itself—but by the willingness to stay open during the crossing. That's what changes us—creating a space inside for a new way of being to emerge.

We are all brave.
We are all remarkable.
We are all sensitive.
We are all worthy.
We are all essential.
We are all incandescent.
We are all blessings.
Even if we forget sometimes.

When I had a terrible self-concept, I could never admit I was imperfect or that I was wrong. My healthy ego was not developed yet, so admitting my shadow was too much to bear. I so wanted to see something good about me, after a childhood of negative feedback. It's important to remember that people often cannot acknowledge their flaws and mistakes, because their self-concepts are not strong enough to handle the admissions. Swimming in a pool of self-hatred, they can't take one more drop of contempt. After years of working through my shame-body—healing it, and proving my value with various achievements, it became a lot easier to admit my shadow characteristics, my mistakes, my arrogance. And, then, because my issues were more transparent, I could actually begin the journey of working them through. This is why the ego-bashing intrinsic to the shadow-avoidant community is a dangerous thing. It confuses people and discourages them from developing the healthy ego necessary to manage reality and value themselves. We need a certain degree of egoic strength to evolve and flourish. Bows to the healthy self-concept. Really.

They tell us to wear masks, repress and hide our true feelings, teach us to adapt our personalities to the marketplace, and then they expect healthy functioning. Is that even possible from below a mask? Can it be any surprise that humans are depressed and act out in hurtful ways when they have been conditioned to distort their truths, bury their feelings, grin and bear it? If we want humans to act empathically, we have to model it to them as a society. If we want humans to stop hurting others, we have to support healthy emotional release so that they do not accumulate toxic feelings. If we want humans to move from their most heartfelt authenticity, we have to stop shaming and shunning their genuine expression. If we want humans to move from love, we must love them first. We can't teach repression and disguise on a society wide level, and then expect loving, compassionate behavior. It's entirely ridiculous.

If all you want is a loveship, shared essence will serve you well. You can meet in the mystic, in the soul-gaze, in the cosmic kiln of mutual divinity. You can ride a twin-flamed magic carpet into eternity, or until it crash lands in denial river, whichever comes first. But if you want a realationship, if you want something that deepens and sustains itself over time, something else is required. Realationships cannot ride on essence alone. They need ground to earth them. They need soul to soil. They need humanness to harvest. They need essence to hoe. Lasting love is not just a question of cosmic chemistry. That's the easy part. Realationships are a soul to sole proposition. We land our loveships on Mama Earth, and begin bridging our purest intentions with our messy humanness. That's the real work.

There is no question in my mind. A state of complete and utter love is our collective birthright; the state we are born to inhabit; the way of being that is eagerly awaiting humanity at the end of a long, perilous journey. We either armor our hearts, or we peel its layers. We either deny our fears, or we confront them. We either walk toward love as a way of being, or we walk away from it. There are only two directions. This decision shapes our life and our world.

Success is finding a way to grow in the heart of a hopeless landscape. To that I bow.

I am not sure where we got the idea that spirituality must be softy toffee gentle and never include anger. This is a perversion of real spirituality, yet another recipe for repression, denial and destruction. This is not to say that all anger is good anger—my spirituality doesn't include unhealthy anger, attacks on innocents, arbitrary judgments, passive aggression. But it does includes healthy anger, justified anger, transformational anger, spiritual activism. In fact, I am certain that we will not create the world of divine possibility that many spiritualists long for, unless we get angry about the injustices that many of us face. There is needless conflict, and there is healthy conflict. The distinction lies in its intentions. It's time to raise healthy anger to the rafters of acceptability in the spiritual community. If you feel that a consciousness model is doing damage to humanity, get angry about it. If you feel that a guru is abusing his authority, get angry about it. If you feel that corporate structures are destroying our planet, get angry about it. There is nothing evolved about repressed expression. Spirituality without conflict isn't spirituality at all. It's a flight from reality. The spiritual activist understands what has to be done. And he does it.

The call of the beloved always comes with the promise of expansion, and seldom in the ways that we imagine. If you want to know what's coming, choose a more practical love. But if you want to grow towards God, let your soul do the picking.

I understand the value of detaching from our pain bodies. Sometimes we need to step back, get some perspective, take a breather. But I also understand that too much detachment, too much transcendence, too much pseudo-presence, will only make things worse for us. If let unattended, the pain-body that we pretended wasn't there will be sure to remind us that it is still within us, growing in size and intensity, turning against us in the form of illness and even death. The masters of dissociation will try to convince us that we are 'in the now' when we bypass our pain, but I can assure you that they are sadly mistaken. That is little more than self-avoidance masquerading as enlightenment. True presence is a whole being experience, one that includes everything we left behind on the path. If we want to really be here now, we have to include the pain-body. And the more work we do to heal it, the less likely we are to be destroyed by it.

Some of us cannot preserve our dignity and well-being if we remain connected to one or both of our parents. This is not to say that we don't do our best to heal and preserve those relationships, but sometimes it is simply not possible and it is not healthy to continue. Unfortunately, many who have made the brave, necessary decision to disconnect are met with a shaming, shunning response from others. It is one of the most destructive and imprisoning guilt trips of all time "But she's your mother", "But he's your father", "They did their best", "You owe them your life." Pay no mind to this. You can be sure that if someone is considering disconnecting from members of their family of origin, there must be very legitimate reasons for doing so. Even if they did their best, that doesn't mean we have to stay in contact with them. Some wounds cut too deep. Some bridges have been permanently burnt. Some people do not change. You are not a bad person if you choose to say good-bye to abusive family members. You have every right to preserve your emotional integrity.

If there is one thing I have grown to understand, it is that resistance is fertile. As long as we are willing to plow its fields with awareness.

If you emerge from the ending of any relationship feeling more positive about yourself; more aware of your rights, needs and entitlements; more celebratory of your magnificence; with a finely attuned authenticity-mometer and better boundaries, then you have had a blessed relationship journey, even if the ending was toxic. The Garden of Heart Knocks yields all manner of fruit.

There are many victims on this planet. Many. And yet it is amazing how determined people can be to deny another's victimhood. Perhaps they are seeking to bypass their own unresolved experiences, or perhaps they have given up on their own healing. Whatever it is, to deny victimhood is to further victimize. And the more we dismiss victimhood, the more we actually perpetuate and enable victimization. I understand that many of us reach a stage where it is essential that we move beyond victimhood, and, in certain situations, recognize how we may have manifested our circumstances. But this is not true for everyone; nor is it true in every situation. For many of us, it is essential that we own our victimhood, that we are seen in our victimhood, and that we do not re-frame our suffering in positive terms, unless and until we feel it is true for us. There is no shame in owning our woundedness. In fact, it may be the only thing that saves us.

When I was young, my sexual encounters were all about me. Like many young male baboons conditioned by a superficial culture, I had a story about how I wanted my lovers to look, to smell, to taste, to walk. If they didn't measure up to my objectifying image, I just wasn't interested. Arrogance! But, my baboon has slowly evolved into an awakening man (not awakenED, but awakenING), one who has grown tired of his limiting story, one who is gradually recognizing that the real turn-on is the one that moves from the inside out. Instead of being turned-on by my fictional story, I am turned on by her actual story—the real life autobiography that her body tells. What was once 'perfect' has no story to tell. What was before 'imperfect', becomes a cornucopia of delight. It's easy to look for God in an unscarred horizon, but what kind of God is that?

Turning to a guru or a spiritual teacher to tell us why we are here is a big mistake, and often, an expensive one. Others can provide us with tools that help us to clear the blockages to clarity, but they cannot tell us which path to walk. That's because our sacred purpose is privately held; it is encoded within us, embodied and embedded, a karmic blueprint that can only be read by the one who carries it. That's why not a single soul on earth can tell us why we are here. They can't decipher a language that is unique to another soul, no matter what claims they make. It's one of the most beautiful things about this human trip: the divine blessed each of us with our own secret lexicon, a unique karmic code that will never be replicated again. We are the book of our life. Now all we have to do is figure out how to read it. One soul page at a time...

I appreciate the value of not turning away from paths and people just because it becomes uncomfortable. We cannot only remain in situations when they feel good because we may have an essential lesson to learn in the heart of the discomfort. At the same time, there seems to be a tendency—in many I know and work with—to forego common sense and remain on unhealthy paths, as if there is some merit in difficulty alone. The idea that all paths and connections carry a seed of transformation feels unhealthy and untrue. There is a meaningful difference between difficult situations that are fodder for expansion, and those where the discomfort is a sign to walk away. This is as true for love relationships as friendships. Sometimes the shadow emerges because we have something to work through. Sometimes it emerges because we are simply not where we belong. Life is so precious. We are only here for a moment. May we meet it with delight.

There are few things more confusing than going to war with a parent who is abusing you, particularly when you are very young. If you fight for your dignity, you risk losing the love that you need from them to develop. If you don't fight back, you lose your self-respect and your development may be delayed. You either have them and lose yourself; or you have you, and further alienate them. How very painful—to have to fight for your right to be here against someone who actually brought you into life. May no more children have to live through that confusion.

It's hard to let someone go when we don't know why they're gone. It's natural to want an explanation, an understanding, something that puts their leaving into perspective. It's hard to move on when there is nothing but silence, or worse, a strangely formal way of relating, as though you made the whole thing up. But we can't put our lives on hold, waiting for an answer that may never come. Maybe they will tell us one day, or maybe they will never understand it themselves. Their reason isn't that important. What is important is that we don't abandon ourselves in the heart of loss. That we don't make another's presence more important than our own. That we don't lock ourselves in a prison of our own making, waiting for an external liberator to set us free. If they have left, we have to leave, too. We have to let the pain through the holes they left behind so it can find its ultimate destination. Our precious life waits on no one.

Excessive analysis perpetuates emotional paralysis. Knowing our issues is not the same as healing our issues. In fact, knowing is often a willful act, entirely incongruent with the experience of surrender required to heal. I have known many who could name their patterns and issues—almost like they had done a science experiment on their own consciousness— but nothing changed because they refused to come back down into their bodies and move their feelings through to transformation. It's safe up there, above the fray, witnessing the pain-body without actually engaging it. The key to the transformation of challenging patterns and wounds is to heal them from the inside out. Not to analyze them, not to watch them like an astronomer staring at a faraway planet through a telescope, but to jump right into the heart of them, encouraging their expression and release, stitching them into new possibilities with the thread of love. You want to become a holy patchwork? Heal your heart.

It is ironic that the greater the love, the more fragile is the patchwork that holds it together. You can pull on practical love connections and they just get stronger. But soulful love tapestries are much more delicate. Holding them together requires great imagination and a willingness to mend the seams time and time again. And regular needles just won't do the job. You need special tools to stand in the heart-fire and re-connect threads of the same divine weave. But what a beautiful heartloom awaits those who can remain devoted to their co-creation.

The inner monsters we distract from are not nearly as dangerous as the monsters we create to avoid them. As painful as early life traumas can be to confront, they are seldom as difficult to transform as the behaviors and addictions that we develop to bypass them. As children, our defenses and distraction techniques saved us, but, as adults, they become a self-fulfilling prophecy, concretizing and locking us in with our early pain, blinding us to the fact that we are now better equipped to work through our memories than we were as children. It may have seemed insurmountable back then, but it no longer is. If we can turn around and face them now, if we can resist the tendency to cover them over with layer upon layer of distortion, we can re-claim our trauma and work it through to resolution. There is no way to run from wound-body memory. It is always there, waiting for its moment of integration. Better to turn around and embrace it. Once a monster, now an opportunity for genuine transformation.

Love needs an entry point. If our emotional body is all blocked up with unresolved material, there's no way in. The more we empty the vessel before it comes, the more space there is for love to flourish. Healing our hearts gives love a place to land.

So many people get judged when they refuse to put their pain away. They get judged for showing it, for speaking it, for insisting on sharing their memories of abuse with those they know. I am not talking about those overwhelming strangers with their stuff—I am talking about legitimate sharings with those they are connected with in daily life. All too often, they are fed one repressive message or another: "Don't look back," "What's done is done," "Don't be a victim," "Your feelings are an illusion," "Be strong." What is ironic about this is that those who insist on embodying and expressing their feelings are actually the courageous ones—unwilling and unable to live a false life. Their stuff is breaking through their defenses because they are tired of carrying the weight of buried truths. They want a healthier and more authentic life. Those who seek to shame their revealings are actually less courageous, turning to repressive mantras in an effort to bypass their own unresolved feelings and memories. If they can shut others down, they can remain shut down themselves. But shut down doesn't take us anywhere good. If we don't deal with our stuff, it deals with us. May we all speak our truths, before our buried truths destroy us. Out with the old, in with the true...

We are often surprised when love falls apart. It makes no sense to us—how can something so beautiful turn so ugly? But we should not be so surprised, because few of us are ready to hold love safe. Few of us are trained in the art of love. The entire world has been organized around masks and defenses. Adaptation and disguise are our specialty. But love is a different world—an unmasked, surrendered landscape that few of us have explored with any great depth. It's easy for most of us to articulate concepts, but to hearticulate feelings is another planet altogether. We are only at the beginning of an enheartened way. We haven't downloaded the ways of the heart. We are learning as we crawl. Best we stop beating ourselves up when it doesn't work out. There is so much left to learn.

It never ceases to amaze me how authors in this field write the wisdoms they most need to read. I write about groundedness, because I have an ungrounded tendency. Many write about being in the now, because they have a tendency to dissociate. Others write about the containment of the ego, because their egos have run amok. Still others write about embodiment, because they can't get out of their heads. We are not great knowers. We are merely travel agents for the particular trip we need to go on. If it calls to you for awhile, you can choose to join us. But never imagine us realized beings—we surely aren't. We are all learning from our mistakes, trying to make sense of it all, walking right beside you on the trailways of transformation...

Forgiveness is not a concept. It's a process. And, if you choose not to forgive at the end of that process, you are not a bad human. No-forgive and forget, works too. It's okay to not forgive in certain situations. It doesn't mean you are not spiritual. It doesn't mean that you are unresolved. It doesn't mean you will come back in the next lifetime to live it out again. The assumption that forgiving the abuser is the benchmark of a completed emotional and karmic process is the mistake. It's another way the New Cage movement insensitively vilifies the victim. The real benchmark of resolution is whether we have gone through our emotional process authentically and have arrived at a place where the negative charge around the experience has dissipated. Perhaps we learned some lesson, or perhaps we just feel liberated from the memories—the important thing is that we feel at peace again. Focusing on our responsibility to forgive a wrongdoer sidetracks the whole process. If it's there, it's there. If it's not, it's not. Just because you don't choose to forgive doesn't mean you haven't let go yet. Maybe you realize forgiveness is not essential to your healing, and not your responsibility. Some of us actually heal and choose not to forgive. Imagine that.

It's not about giving up on the fairy tale relationship. It's about landing it in reality. It's about giving the fairy feet. It's about peeling away the prince's armor and loving the human down below. It's about wiping off the princess' make-up and loving her divine humanness. It's about finding romance in the naked fires of daily life. When our masks and disguises fall away, real love can reveal itself. Forget fairy tales— the human tale is much more satisfying. We just have to learn how to get turned-on by humanness.

We have been handed the blessing of a lifetime. It's called life. If only we knew what a gift it is, we wouldn't waste a single second hating, hurting, distracting, fleeing the fires of self-creation. No, no, we would be down on our knees, worshiping the gift, unpacking the treasure, not missing a moment's opportunity to give praise. So much energy is wasted on bloody nonsense. I want to worship. Please join me.

I saw someone crying in public recently. It was genuinely beautiful, honest, natural. I felt the impulse to walk over and comfort her, but my deeper instinct was to leave her be. She didn't seem to be suffering. She seemed to be liberating from whatever was bothering her. And then someone—a relative, perhaps—came over and hugged her, before handing her a bunch of tissues. The whole energy changed, as the crier wiped her nose and face and stopped crying. On one level, it looked sweet—a caring person coming over to comfort them—but, on another, it looked repressive, even shaming. The tissues come with their own inherent message: "This is too messy. Let's clean that up and put it away. God forbid the world should know you are feeling pain." It's sad but true—that's how much we value emotional authenticity in this world: tissues come before heartfelt release. For all the tissue-bearer knew, that release was going to save her from tremendous future suffering. It's time to turn things right-side up. Better a little messy now, than the big messy that comes from repressed feelings later. Clearing first, tissues later. Let the river flow.

I feel startled and infuriated by those who call people who commit suicide "cowards." It is the height of arrogance and insensitivity to imagine ourselves judges over a person's decision to stay or to go. Only the individual knows what trauma they are carrying, what pain they have known, what darkness blankets their inner world, what courage it has taken to stay even this long. Only the individual soul knows what path it is here to walk, and when its time has come. If you are lucky enough to have never considered suicide in this challenging world, then get down on your knees and thank your lucky stars. Really, get down and kiss the ground and give thanks. But do not judge those who have made a different choice. But for the grace of God go you...

The idea that there is an interface between our thoughts and a responsive universe is a vast improvement over the belief that we are alone down here, and that no one is listening. But the suggestion that all we have to do is change our thinking is a backward step that has led many astray. It's not that easy. We have to do the deeper work to actually alter our consciousness. The universe doesn't respond to feigned positivity, flights of fancy, starry-eyed imaginings with little ground to support them. The universe responds to authentic expansion. I have known too many good souls who lost their footing by buying into the wishful thinking movement. Many of them lost everything while chasing a dream before they had built the necessary foundation to manifest and sustain it. It is time to ground our spirituality in good ole common sense. There are no magic potions on the trailways of transformation. One foot in front of the other, one learning at a time, from sole to soul.

It's so ironic. Many of us chase the approval of those that don't value us, while ignoring those that do. We put so much energy into impressing people with our appearance and achievements, and they pay attention for ten seconds and then go back to eating their lunch. All the energy that gets put into gaining external validation is fruitless, until we find a way to impress ourselves. And when we do finally learn to love ourselves, we are too busy living a self-loving life to care what others think about us.

While I am a great advocate for owning and healing our shadow, I also recognize the value of doing all we can to find the light where possible. Not the pseudo-light, but the light of true-path, the light of hope, the light of love. I have known a great many individuals who clung to the darkness like a security blanket, cloaking their fear of the light beneath perpetual processing and victim-hood. The darkness bypass. It is one thing to open the shadow treasure-chest in an effort to heal and become more authentic. It is quite another to hide in the shadows and make it our home. May we never forget that once the lights turn off in this life, they are probably staying off for a very long time. Best not to glorify the darkness. Once we have done enough work around the shadow, we have a choice. We can either open it to darkness, or we can open it to light. Trauma, or treasure? It's up to you.

Just because we have a kind of 'soul feeling' with someone doesn't mean we should always explore it. It doesn't mean we should jump on in, even if we are hungry for that kind of connection. Because resonance alone does not tell you if the path is going to be an additive one, any more than synchronicity tells you which way to walk. Sometimes it is an invitation to expansion, and sometimes it is nothing but trouble. Sometimes it's a call to other, and sometimes it's a calling to parts of the self that are ready to come alive. We have to trust our intuition, and we have to practice the art of conscious discernment, especially when the synchronicity bell chimes the loudest. If it's really meant to be, it will reveal itself as true in time.

We need to compassion-eyes this planet. For real. Not simply to talk about all-oneness, but to bring it into everyday life. To walk past a homeless person and to really be with them. To hear a friend's story of suffering and to be fully present with it. To bring those into our heart who need refuge. To inconvenience our lives in an effort to help up someone in need. Let's walk together, side by side. We are all struggling to get here before it's time to go. Compassion for our shared struggle is the way home.

The pace of our process is as important as anything on the heroic journey to true-path. All too often, I encounter individuals who beat themselves up because they haven't found their callings yet. They have caught a glimpse of where they want to be, they have heard their truth-aches signaling that they are not where they belong, but they aren't quite ready to make the leap. This is not to say that we don't need a push now and then, but it is to say that we have to be realistic about the process. This is a world organized around survivalism—not authenticity—so we are always going against the cultural grain when we quest for true-path. Foraging through the forests of artifice to find an authentic clearing is no easy feet. It takes courage, and it also takes time. One soul step after another...

I want to leave a positive karmic footprint. Not a perfectly shaped one, not one that walked the clearest path, but one that authentically reflects my soul's distinct journey. No doubt it will be a little rough around the edges, perhaps even heavily scarred from years of hard traveling; but that's okay, as long as it heals and smooths over time, leaving more and more love in its wake. I never imagined life an easy saunter, but if I can continue to wander with a giving heart, I will leave a footprint to be proud of, one where sole meets soul on sacred footpaths. I want to cast my eyes on a beautiful footprint, before it is time to go.

Those who feel like the darkness is overwhelming: Keep the faith. You are surely not alone. We are all stumbling for the light switch. We must share any light we find.

Love. What are we waiting for? It's all we're going to remember, at the end of it. Love with all your heart.

♡

Apologies to the Battered Child
(from a parent in process)

Note: I wrote this piece around my 50th birthday, imagining the letter my inner child would liked to have received from my parents.

I apologize for beating you with my fists and feet when you were small and vulnerable. I apologize for wounding your body temple. I apologize for burning your hands, breaking your finger, scarring your flesh. I simply couldn't see you, lying there in a pool of blood and sorrow. Blinded by my own repressed rage, I saw an easy mark for my aggression. I saw a new host for my pain. I now understand that my abusiveness was a smokescreen for my own woundedness. A habit entrenched early in life, it felt easier to repeat the abuse than to heal it. And, in many ways, your aliveness reminded me of my own deadness—I had to shut you down so I could remain asleep. Beneath it all, I had so much love for you, my sweet child. I just couldn't manifest it. I don't ask for your forgiveness—you must be true to your own process first—but I do ask that you grant yourself permission to heal and to live a life that is liberated from my effects.

I apologize for attempting to dim your beautiful light. It was so bright that it threatened my own unmet need for attention—who would notice me, in your enlivened presence? Although I was chronologically older than you when you were born, I was actually emotionally regressed, trapped in an unhealed primal consciousness that ruled my behavior. I had grown up in a family of love-starved narcissists, each of us clamoring to see our individual reflections in a too tiny pool of validation. With our lights hidden under a bushel of shame, no one ever felt seen. Stealing other people's light became my misguided path of self-elevation, a misplaced attempt at boosting my diminished self-concept. I am so sorry for this attack on the integrity of your being. You had every right to embody your magnificence with dignity. You had every right to shine.

I apologize for vilifying and scapegoating you. I am sorry that I actively blamed you for my own misery. I couldn't hold my self-hatred any longer—I needed to pass it on to someone else. You were the perfect recipient for my frustration—you couldn't defend yourself. And, I remember the worst of it—telling you that my life would have been better if you had died, instead of the daughter I lost. As I read these words, I find myself almost turning away from your picture—it is too much to imagine that I could leave you with that—but I stay and face your image. I face it not because I can change what I have done, but because I owe it to you to stay in the fire of my own regret.

I apologize for mocking you and repeatedly calling you names. I should have known the scars that insults leave on a vulnerable being—mockery was fundamental to my family dynamics. In the heat of desperate survivalism, insulting each other was a momentary relief from our chronic state of hopelessness. I am sorry for perpetuating that pattern at your expense. I only wish I could reach inside of you and take back the words I left there. I know that you internalized many of those insults and believed them to be true. I know that it shaped your lens. Please know that my message was entirely my own stuff. Please know that you are beautiful in my eyes. And, more importantly, please know that you are beautiful through your own eyes. Please heal the remnants of my madness.

I apologize for turning others against you and pitting you against your own siblings. Lodged in a competitive world view, my reality was divided into territories—threats and protections, enemies and friends, them and us. The demons of duality—ne'er the twain shall meet. Through this fearful lens, differences were equated with threats to survival rather than opportunities for learning. Like snorting animals on the prowl, if you didn't behave like us, you were the enemy. Because you were so different from the rest of us, I identified you as an enemy. I forgot our biological connection, our shared humanness, our karmic engagement. I forgot the bridge that existed between our hearts.

I am so deeply sorry that I left you alone in your developing years. I apologize for abandoning you when you needed me most. I remember your cries for contact, your tireless efforts to connect, your tearful eyes through the living room window as I drove away. I looked away, but I still felt you. I just couldn't do anything about it. In many ways, I confused you with the bad marriage that produced you, a marriage that I desperately longed to escape from. When I had you, I was so emotionally immature. There was so little space inside me for another person's needs. As I grow into my real adulthood, I am able to empathize with your heartbreak. In the last years, I have spent much time growing into the parent you deserved. Please know that I have taken that journey seriously.

I want you to know that I see you more clearly now. I see the fear that I left you with. I see the ways that it impacted your life choices, emotional availability, patterns of self-distraction. I see the ways that self-doubt prevented you from fully owning your power. Despite my madness, some part of me noticed the ways that you shut down to cope: the shallowing of your breath, the armoring of your heart, the reluctance to be seen. But I also see the ways that you overcame. I see the ways that you championed your own cause. I see the ways that you converted your fear into hope. I see how hard you worked to grow yourself. I am proud of you in ways that words can never express.

Most of the greatest achievements on the planet are unknown to others—private overcomings, silent attempts at belief, re-opening a shattered heart. The real path of champions truly lies within: the transforming of suffering into expansion, the clearing of horrifying debris, the building of a healthy self-concept without tools. The greatest achievers have found a way to believe in something good despite being traumatized and fractured on life's battlefields. You are one of them. You overcame me. No matter what else you accomplish in your life, you are already a Champion.

I am grateful that you disconnected from me many years ago instead of coming back for more abuse. You realized that I couldn't meet your parental needs and that you had to look elsewhere. You were so very right. By choosing to protect yourself, you also created the conditions for my own transformation. In your absence, in your determined refusal to enable my patterns, I was forced to recognize my impact. At first, I resisted the learning, but the love I felt for you penetrated my defenses and left me with no other option but to do the work. That work took me far back in time—both to our time together and to my own early life. Ah, the Power of Then—the impact of unresolved feelings on our now consciousness. Try as I did to disarm them by witnessing them, it was entirely ineffective. You cannot heal and resolve your emotional material with your mind. Your emotional material does not evaporate because you watch it. You can only heal your heart with your heart. I had no choice but to go back down the path and re-claim my feelings. In this way, you were my greatest teacher: the one who gave me back my heart.

Over the years, my own emotional armor has melted away. I have lost the energy that I once had to distract from my truth. I have grown tired of my falsity, denials and projections. And something has grown within me: a willingness to see what I have done and to acknowledge where I have failed. I don't know if I will have another incarnation to do it better, but I want to set a loving intention before I die. I want to be living in truth when I close my eyes on this lifetime. And some part of the truth is horrifying to me. I know what I have done. I know the violence in my heart. And I know the causal factors: the desperate survivalism that plagued my family line, the shutting down of my emotional current, the build-up of resentment. But I also know that I had a choice. I could hear the voice of love calling me away during those acts of violence. But I chose to continue. I was influenced by my childhood, but I alone chose my path. Before God and before you, I am accountable for those choices.

As our society crosses the bridge from survivalism to authenticity as our way of being, I have every faith that one day, we will move from love. I have done it, and I feel confident that others will follow. As part of that process, I call on all bullies to step out of their comfort zone and make determined efforts to shift their abusive paradigm. To find the courage to face the source of their rage. To break the lineage of toxic conditioning. To find constructive ways to soften their edges. To steer the collective (un)consciousness in new directions. To learn healthy ways to channel their aggression. Don't do it only for those who you are harming. Do it for yourself as well. There is no life with a closed heart.

I do not know how God will judge me. I do not know how you will judge me. I do know that I have done all I can to own my actions and to open my heart. I am on my knees before truth. Know that I understand if you choose to remain disconnected. I truly do. You have to be true to your own process. But also know that I am here for you if ever you choose to open the gate again. Nearly 50 years late, but the way is clear.

—J.B., 2012

"Thank you, I Love You"
An Exercise in Self-Love
Created by Jeff Brown

We all have been wounded in the course of our lives: painful childhood experiences, challenging parents, an unkind environment. Sometimes our inner voice can be our harshest critic, carrying the imprint of our prior experiences. It is no easy thing to shift, but it can transform over time, particularly if we are determined in our efforts to consolidate a new way of relating to ourselves. Such tender healing can happen when we change the voice of our inner self—from a critical tone to a tenor of kindness, gentleness, and love. This exercise will help you hold hands with your self again. I invite you to do it often, even if it feels uncomfortable, until it feels right.

You can do this exercise lying down, or looking at yourself in the mirror. You can be clothed or naked. You can also do it in the shower or bathtub.

This exercise invites you to thoroughly touch your body, all of it. Touch yourself with as much presence as you can. Be slow and gentle with the process—don't rush. Be fully here for each part of this exercise, intimately feel your own contact, really hear and feel your words.

If you are not comfortable doing this in reality, try doing it as a meditation, getting into a relaxed state and imagining yourself going through the same steps. Or, if you don't feel prepared to imagine yourself expressing this love to yourself just yet, imagine it being expressed to you by someone you care about, or by a presence or guide.

And remember that you can do this exercise as often as you want. Each time will be different. Be aware of what comes up in the experience. Be aware of any voices that attempt to undermine the message. Be aware of them, and do your best to continue.

Begin by using your right hand to touch your left hand. Touch it as lovingly as you can, with gentle strokes. Say out loud, "Thank you, I love you." Now use your left hand to touch your right hand in the same way. Say out loud, "Thank you, I love you."

Now use one or both hands to touch your head. Say out loud, "Thank you, I love you." And touch your nose. Say out loud, "Thank you, I love you." Your eyes. Say out loud, "Thank you, I love you." Your ears. Say out loud, "Thank you, I love you." Your face. Take time with your face, caressing it with great care, letting it know that its authenticity is valued. As you touch, imagine any masks melting away—revealing your vulnerable true face, beneath. Say out loud "Thank you, I love you."

Now move your left hand over your right arm and shoulder. Say out loud, "Thank you, I love you." Now move your right hand over your left arm and shoulder. Say out loud, "Thank you, I love you."

Now put both hands on your neck and your chest, caressing them with kindness. Place your hands over your lungs. Rest them there for a moment, feeling the breath of life rising and falling. Say out loud, "Thank you, I love you." Now put one or both hands over your heart. Feel the beat of life. Let yourself feel it speaking to you, let it remind you that you are here for a reason. Say out loud "Thank you, I love you." The heart loves to feel gratitude.

Now run one or both hands over your stomach and your organs. Again, take your time. Self-love has no time constraints. Feel into the magnificence of your human body—all the functions that happen outside of your conscious awareness, all the millions of ways the body regenerates and enlivens you, all the millions of ways it echoes your value. Really let yourself feel its love for you. Say out loud, "Thank you, I love you." Say it as many times as you need before you can really feel it.

Now move one or both hands to your genitals.

Experience the wonder of creation that lies there. The sacred pleasure centers. As you touch, let yourself open past any sense of shame—into pure wonder. Touch yourself with kindness, gratitude and compassion. Say out loud, "Thank you, I love you."

Now move one or both hands down your legs. Caress your legs—they work so hard and so seldom get affection. Give them affection. Say out loud, "Thank you, I love you."

Now move to your feet. Touch your toes. Rub your hands over the bottom of your feet. Tickle them. Stroke the tops of your feet. Your ankles. Your shins. Massage the whole area. As you do, say out loud, "Thank you, I love you."

Now touch your buttocks, with affection. It's not easy to be sat on for hours per day. :) Give them some lovin'. Say out loud, "Thank you, I love you."

Reach up for your kidneys. Rub your hands over them. They are such hard workers. Let them feel your gratitude. Say out loud, "Thank you, I love you."

Now touch some part of your back. Massage and stroke it with gratitude and affection. Say out loud, "Thank you, I love you."

Now rest your hands for a moment. Either look in a mirror, or imagine yourself in your mind's eye. Look at yourself before you: all of you, the you that God(dess) created, the you that came into being, the you that is breathed by the universe, the you that is still here, the you that has overcome, the you that has found the faith to go on, the authentic you that lives below the world's disguises...

And say aloud, "Thank you, I love you. Thank you, I love you. Thank you, I love you, Thank you..."

Sacred Dynamite

I have never been one who believed that human births are accidents, or that we are little more than random concentrations of stardust. I believe we are all here with a divine purpose at the heart of our birth. As we deal with the challenges, pressures and distractions of daily life, it is all too easy to lose sight of this purpose and become spiritually unimaginative, momentarily forgetting that there is a wellspring of magnificence lying in wait within us. This week, I invite you to remember.

My divine purpose first appeared like a distant flute, hints and whispers of something deeper that called to me in the night. And then it became clearer, a little voice that whispered sweet somethings in my inner ear whenever I dared to walk a false path.

I heard it when I was planning to open a law practice, involved in an unhealthy relationship, sitting in traffic on the way to work: "No, not that way Jeffrey, walk this way." Although it challenged my seeming stability, the voice had an odd sense of authority to it, as though it carried the blueprint for a karmic destiny I had long forgotten. The little voice that knows...

I somehow trusted this voice and followed it home, embarking on an intense spiritual journey through challenging emotional and economic terrain. Fifteen years later, with trial law long behind me, I found myself in the back room of my house writing a book I was destined to write. As I wrote, my soul's voice rose to the rafters of consciousness and I learned that who I had previously identified as "Jeff" was only a small part of my story. Beneath my misidentifications was an essential self, bridged to deeper callings and eternal rhythms. The voice was right. I had found my way to true-path, my in-power point, my place of purpose and meaning.

At the heart of every human birth is such a place. In my book Soulshaping, I use the term "soul-scriptures" to describe the callings, lessons and archetypal pathways that live at the heart of our transformation. By excavating and honoring these scriptures, we expand our souls one step closer to the Godself.

Although the ultimate romance is with our own soul, it is our experiences together that give birth to the essential lessons. We join together in a dance of sacred imagination, stepping on each other's toes and turning each other toward God one clumsy step after another. If one of us steps off the dance floor, we postpone others' lessons too.

This week I ask you to believe that you are needed for what you bring, and to never lose faith in your brilliance, no matter what the world sends your way. Although it is all too easy to forget, the Divine Mother continues to breathe you because you are essential here. She would take you back in a soul-beat if you had no role here. Our divine purpose may be hidden from view, it may be covered in dust, but it's still in there, sparkling with infinite possibility, waiting in the wings for its opportunity to humanifest.

We may have to work hard to bring it to light, but we must never give up on our profound nature. Below the surface, we are all sacred dynamite, waiting for that just right spark to ignite our divine purpose. Once ignited, we explode into a realm of unlimited possibility. What seemed profound before, becomes just the tip of the soulberg. When you are ready, look inside and your magnificence will rise to the surface on the wings of the inner dove. I tell you, it's that close.

(from Jeff's ABC 'Good Morning America'
Inspiration collection- January 22, 2010)

Truth Mountain

In the early years of my Soulshaping journey, I had a constant desire to be "in the moment." I didn't quite know what that meant, but I knew that there was some connection between my capacity to be fully present for the moment and my ultimate spiritual expansion. If I couldn't be here, how could I possibly grow to the next place on my journey?

I looked for the moment everywhere. I hunted for it on the yoga mat, the meditation cushion, the Bioenergetic breathing stool. I sought it through detachment practices, depth-full adventures, emotional clearings, mantra and tantra. All Go(o)d, but something was missing.

What was missing was truth. We often talk about living in the moment but it is my experience that we cannot live fully in the moment if we are not living in truth. Truth is the gateway to the moment. Without truth, our breaths are somehow incomplete, our presence shrouded, our intimacy half-hearted because we are not fully there for it. The moment we own our truths, we get truth-chills—little sighs of relief from our body temple—as the veils to clarity fall away and our divine presence enters. Here we are. Here now.

Of course, truth is a subjective experience. What is

one person's truth is another person's falsity. For me, truth is that which reflects my own distinct soul-scriptures—those callings, lessons and archetypal pathways that live at the heart of my spiritual expansion. To the extent that I am honoring my scriptures, I am on my true-path and in the moment. When I bypass them, I am somewhere else entirely. For me, no spiritual practice is effective unless I am courageously honoring my path.

It took me a long time to realize that there were symptoms of my alienation from true-path. They included chronic illness, sleeplessness, self-distractive behavior, and perpetual dissatisfaction. I took to calling these symptoms "truth-aches"—nudging feelings of falsity, palpable longings for an authentic life. Although sometimes painful, and although embracing them may well force us to turn our habitual patterns upside-down in order to effect change, truth-aches actually contain the seeds of our transformation. When we repress them, truth decay sets in and the only thing that can save us is a truth canal. Sometimes we wait too long, and we lose our truth altogether.

My truth-aches were most evident in my emotional life. When I was repressing old hurts—anger, grief, shame—I felt disconnected from the moment. I would sit on the meditation cushion and feel nothing but agitation. My consciousness was still back there. In my first book *Soulshaping: A Journey of Self-Creation*, I call this "The Power of Then"—the effect the past has on our present-day awareness. Although the physical body travels forward chronologically, our emotional consciousness lingers at any point of departure. To come fully into the moment, we have to go back and deal with the wounds and memories that obstruct us. Not get lost in them, but own them and work them through to the lessons they contain. We have to be there then, before we can be here now.

This week, I encourage you to contemplate your relationship to truth, particularly with regards to your personal relationships and your daily pursuits. What does "true-path" mean to you? Are you embodying your truths? Do you hear a nagging voice calling you in another direction... or do you have peace with path?

Lately I think of truth as a magnificent white-tipped Mountain. At its peak is a deeper and more inclusive experience of the moment. As we move through our lives, Truth Mountain comes in and out of view, calling out to us and reminding us of what is possible. The more honest we are about our path, the higher our consciousness climbs. When our view is blocked, we know that we still have work to do in the valleys down below: traversing the foothills of illusion, sidestepping the quicksands of artifice, overcoming our fear of (interior) heights. But we will get to the peak, if we are willing to do the work, if we can be truthful with ourselves about the ways we avoid the truth.

Something magical happens when we excavate and honor our truth, however one chooses to define it. It doesn't matter how much we achieve or how many things we master, if we are not walking our true-path. The moment we lie to ourselves, we leave the moment. The bridge across the river lie is ever-tempting—it still tempts me often—but there is nothing for us there. When we shed our cloaks of falsity and shamelessly embody our truths, the God-Gate opens and our Essence steps on through. Truth is the gateway to the moment. Honest.

(from Jeff's ABC 'Good Morning America'
Inspiration collection- March 19, 2010)

Enrealment: A New 'Weastern' Consciousness

Throughout my tumultuous early life, I found comfort in blissful and perfectionist imaginings. In an effort to escape the chaos of my family environment, I fixed my gaze on visions of a self-actualized reality, one where the world I inhabited would be in a state of perfect order. This vision served me for many years, until I made the mistake of projecting it onto my spiritual life—manifested as a misguided quest for 'enlightenment.' I soon learned.

Although enlightenment has been broadly defined in the spiritual literature, it is often interpreted as a kind of pure consciousness; a 'heightened' and purified state of being that is detached from our everyday concerns. In its own way, this interpretation can actually lead us away from the karmic field of expansion itself: our daily life. It is only through a growing interface with our real-life experiences and challenges—the School of Heart Knocks—that we can evolve towards a deeper spiritual life.

With this in mind, I invite you to consider a more grounded approach this week, one that reflects what I have realized on my own Soulshaping journey. Enrealment is the quest for a more inclusive consciousness, one that makes no distinction between our spiritual and earthly lives. Through the eyes of enrealment, the more spiritual person lives in all aspects of reality simultaneously—the emotional, the material, and the subtle realms—rather than only those realms that feel the most comfortable, or the most 'elevated.' Our quest is not simply to live in the light—as enlightenment implies—but is to be more genuinely here in all respects: shadow and light, earth and sky, grocery list and unity consciousness. By living in the real, our experience of the moment becomes more complete, our ascension more true.

Enrealment means that we recognize the chaotic magnificence of our daily life as intrinsic to our spirituality. It means seeing the Godself in our connection to the world around us: Everything is God, God is Everything. It means consciously seeking a "Weastern" Consciousness—a consciousness that weaves the quest for unity that is fundamental to the east with the quest for emotional health and a healthy self-concept intrinsic to the west. It means honoring our physical form not simply as a 'vessel' for the soul, but as the embodiment of the soul. It means learning how to connect with our bodies as gardens of truth. It means calling ourselves on our detachment from our shadow. It means honoring our personal experiences as our own built-in learning channel. It means shifting our perspective. What is on one level a challenge, is simultaneously an opportunity for expanding our consciousness.

Enrealment also includes doing the often difficult work needed to clear our emotional debris and work through our most pressing issues. Repressed emotions are unactualized spiritual lessons. We clear our emotional debris both because it creates space inside for our authentic self to emerge and express itself, and because inherent in those feelings and memories are the lessons we need to grow in our spirituality. By bringing our repressed emotions to the surface and working them through, we expand our "soulular" consciousness. By growing down, we grow up...

In "chakric" terms, enrealment means we begin at the beginning. We begin with an honoring of our root chakra—the quest for OM begins at home—and work our way up from there, one chakra after another. It is not enough for our feet to merely skim the ground. Our spiritual life begins with our feet planted firmly on Mother Earth. With our soles firmly planted, our soul has a leg to stand on in its efforts to go higher. Ascending with both feet on the ground.

As we work through our chakras, we become organically present in our bodies and in the moment.

From this delightful presence emerges a natural and sustainable movement toward God. Instead of settling for the occasional enlightenment moment, we are now capable of a more heightened way of being. One we can actually sustain. One we can actually ground into. From sole to soul...

(from Jeff's ABC 'Good Morning America'
Inspiration collection- July 8, 2010)

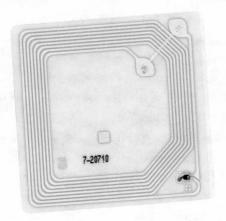

About the Author

A former criminal lawyer and psychotherapist, Jeff Brown is the author of 4 previous books: *Soulshaping: A Journey of Self-Creation, Ascending with Both Feet on the Ground, Love it Forward,* and *An Uncommon Bond.* He is also the author of the viral blog *Apologies to the Divine Feminine* (from a warrior in transition) and the producer, and key journeyer in the award-winning spiritual documentary *Karmageddon,* which also stars Ram Dass, Seane Corn, David Life, Deva Premal and Miten. He has written a series of inspirations for ABC's Good Morning America and appeared on over 200 radio shows. His first book of quotes, *Ascending with Both Feet on the Ground,* was published in the autumn of 2012. Endorsed by best-selling authors

Elizabeth Lesser, Oriah Mountain Dreamer and Katherine Woodward Thomas, 'Ascending' is a collection of some of Jeff's most popular spiritual graffiti—quotes, soul-bytes and aphorisms—frequently shared in social media. His second book of quotes, Love it Forward, was published on Valentine's day, 2014. Endorsed by best-selling authors Caroline Myss and Andrew Harvey, 'Love' contains many of Jeff's most popular love and relationship quotes. His higher consciousness love story 'An Uncommon Bond', was published in May, 2015 to sparkling reviews. 'Bond' is also available as an audio book, through Blackstone Audio. *Spiritual Graffiti* is the third in his series of quotes books. Jeff is also the founder of Enrealment Press and the creator of a new online school, Soulshaping Institute, which launched in January, 2015. He is presently in Toronto, working on a book that reflects his lens on spirituality. You can connect with Jeff's work at www.soulshaping.com, www.soulshapinginstitute.com and www.enrealment.com.